Christian Mission and Islamic Da'wah

Proceedings of the Chambésy Dialogue Consultation

The Islamic Foundation

© The Islamic Foundation 1982/1402 H.

ISBN 0 86037 110 7

Views expressed by different authors of books and studies published by the Islamic Foundation do not necessarily represent the views of the Islamic Foundation.

Published by
The Islamic Foundation
223 London Road
Leicester, UK

Qu·an House
P.O. Box 30611, Nairobi, Kenya

PMB 3193, Kano, Nigeria

British Library CIP data
Chambésy Dialogue Consultation *(1976)*
    Christian mission and Islamic da'wah.
    1. Islam-Relations-Christianity — Congresses
    2. Missions to Muslims — Congresses
    I. Title
    248.2'46   BV2625

    ISBN 0-86037-110-7

Printed in Great Britain by
NENE LITHO
Earls Barton, Northamptonshire

Bound by
WOOLNOUGH BOOKBINDING
Wellingborough, Northamptonshire

CONTENTS

FOREWORD

The relationship between Christians and Muslims is not a new phenomenon. It is a fact of life, even more today than perhaps decades or centuries ago.

Christian-Muslim dialogue, although an important dimension of these relations, is however but one of its aspects and Muslims feel that Christian mission among Muslims overshadows dialogue everywhere. This issue places great strain upon the overall relationship between Christians and Muslims. To the best of my knowledge, the 1976 Chambésy Consultation on *'Christian Mission and Islamic Da'wah'* is the only occasion where in Christian-Muslim dialogue this issue has not only been made the agenda but has been discussed with considerable frankness. Neither before nor since have 'mission and *da'wah'* been placed into the limelight of dialogue.

The Islamic Foundation's decision to reprint the proceedings of the conference first published as the October 1976 issue, Vol. LXV, of the *International Review of Mission* was spurred by at least three considerations:

1. because of its agenda, the Chambésy Consultation to which the Islamic Foundation's Chairman, Professor Khurshid Ahmad, contributed substantially, continued to interest both Muslims and non-Muslims and requests for briefings could best be answered by supplying the published conference proceedings.

2. because of its agenda, the Chambésy Consultation is in fact a milestone on the very long road through the area of Christian-Muslim relations, from worse to better, and an outstanding event. As such it needs documentation, and information about it must not be confined to the archives and files of specialised institutions and libraries.

3. because the issues debated at Chambésy have not been resolved, circulation of the proceedings on a wide scale should also serve as a reminder to both Christians and Muslims that what was discussed between them as early as 1976 needs implementation, perhaps even more urgently now.

Of course one could not expect the issues to be resolved immediately and completely, but there was hope for some significant development. At least signs for coming change were to be expected. The 'Statement of the Conference' informed all those of us interested in or even involved in Christian-Muslim dialogue that such signs were envisaged by the participants. Among them were the call to 'Christian churches and religious organisations to suspend their misused *diakonia* activities in the world of Islam' (No. 7), and the invitation 'to an assembly representative of the two faiths to consider the methods of mission and *da'wah,* and the rules pertinent to each religion, and to seek modalities for enabling each religion to exercise its missionary call/*da'wah* in accordance with its own faith' (No. 8).

5

However, we all know that we are far from this, perhaps further away than in 1976. Christians and Muslims have *not* — since 1976 — continued their debate on mission and *da'wah* in order to improve their relations, at least not in the manner envisaged by the Chambésy participants. The misused *diakonia* activities in the world of Islam not only have *not* been discontinued, but in fact *expanded* since 1976, on a vast scale and with the knowledge and participation of the very same institutions whose members were participants in Chambésy. Just one example may suffice: a multi-million dollar campaign has since been launched to evangelise the Fulani Muslims all over West Africa, and this with the knowledge and participation of all major church bodies, although mainly supported by the Lutheran Churches.* Such developments do not help to ease the tensions that exist between Christians and Muslims everywhere, and this was pointed out in Chambésy in 1976. Today, more than five years later, it needs to be re-emphasised and all participants in Christian-Muslim dialogues, both Christians and Muslims, need to be reminded that the issue of Christian missionary work among Muslims is of greatest concern to us and should no longer be ignored. It is here where a change in relationships must develop and it is to this, among other issues, that the 'Christian Mission and Islamic *Da'wah*' consultation pointed strongly.

It is with the hope that the Conference message will bear more fruit in future, that we have included the republication of its proceedings into the Islamic Foundation's programme of 'Studies in Christian-Muslim Relations'. We gratefully acknowledge the permission for reprint granted by the editorial board of the *International Review of Mission.*

We pray to Allah that He may accept this humble effort of ours to contribute to the increase of understanding and the decrease of tensions and mistrust between Christians and Muslims.

Leicester,   Ahmad von Denffer
9th December, 1981

* For details see Denffer, Ahmad von : *The Fulani Evangelism Project in West Africa,* Leicester: The Islamic Foundation, 1980.

EDITORIAL

Islam and Christianity are missionary faiths; among the adherents of both there is a desire to share the riches of the faith and the heritage with others. But it is notorious that, in the attempt to fulfill this missionary vocation, missionary activities of Christians among Muslims, and of Muslims among Christians, have sometimes led to grievances on both sides; both groups have long memories of past pressures to conform or more recent experiences of aggressive and insensitive proselytism.

With the unhappy events in the Lebanon and Mindinao and the growing tensions in other parts of the world demonstrating how urgent it is today to create conditions of understanding and mutual respect, we felt that the least we could do was to try to contribute to the elimination of the religious passions which further enflame conflicts basically due, much of the time, to economic, ideological or political differences.

On June 26th, with the cooperation of the two co-convenors, Dr David Kerr, Director of the Centre for the Study of Islam and Christian-Muslim Relations and Lecturer in Islam at the Selly Oak Colleges, Birmingham, and a sympathetic student of Islam, and Professor Khurshid Ahmad, Leicester, Director General of the Islamic Foundation, formerly professor of economics at the University of Karachi and a man well-acquainted with the Christian world, we called together a group of Christians and Muslims concerned with the fulfilment of their respective missionary obligations for a five-day consultation on Christian Mission and Islamic *Da'wah*.

We as Christians cannot surrender our missionary vocation nor our commitment to the proclamation of the Gospel. But the same missionary compulsion to engagement in *da'wah* belongs to our Muslim neighbours out of their own religious heritage and from their religious convictions. The group tried to explain to each other their basic motivations, to understand and if possible to correct the caricatures they had of one another, and to see how damaging realities could be changed and a pattern of behaviour in mission and *da'wah* defined and commended. The encounter was an impassioned one, in which it was not easy to agree. At the same time, however, time and time again, we came back to the conference table with the conviction that ways could and should be found to create more fruitful situations for reciprocal witness.

Working on a draft prepared originally by the Muslim participants, the group was able to hammer out a general expression of agreement. This document might have reflected other approaches to the matter — more radical, or more daring, or more conservative. But its value lies in the fact that it is not just an expression of our Christian understanding of how mission could or should be carried out among adherents of the Muslim religion, or vice versa, but that together, Christians and Muslims affirmed basic principles concerning the freedom to exercise one's religion, to propagate one's faith, "the right to convince and be convinced" and deplored those things which stand in the way of the exercise of such freedom.

For me, who had had little previous contact with Muslims and the world of Islam, the discussions, the papers and not least the human contacts were an illuminating experience. We believe that you will find much to think about in this issue of the IRM. Now the editorial word belongs to our two friends, and the co-editors of this issue, Khurshid Ahmad and David Kerr.

EMILIO CASTRO

ⵎⵎⵎⵎⵎⵎⵎⵎⵎⵎⵎⵎⵎⵎⵎⵎⵎⵎⵎⵎⵎⵎⵎⵎⵎⵎⵎⵎⵎⵎⵎⵎ

In the name of Allah, the Merciful, the Mercy-Giving.

> SAY: "People of the Book, (let us) rally to common terms, to be binding on both, us and you, that we shall worship only God (alone) and associate nothing else with Him, nor shall any of us take others as lords instead of God".

The Qur'ān 3 : 64

Perhaps this is the first time that a Muslim has acted as a co-editor for a special issue of the IRM. On the face of it, this may appear to be a small step, yet it may go a long way in improving the state of religious co-existence: moving from co-existence towards pro-existence and greater co-operation between the family of Abraham (peace be upon him). The initiative for the present effort

8

came from the Commission on World Mission and Evangelism of the World Council of Churches and the IRM, to which the Muslims have responded in good faith.

After working on this project for almost one year, I, for one, have no regrets for having entered these uncharted waters. We met and worked together as people committed to serve God alone, and as persons resolved to live in accordance with the religious values and traditions we firmly believe in. We hold no brief for syncretism, nor were we interested in producing compromises on matters religious and moral. Similarly, we did not enter the consultation with a view to scoring points on each other. We met with the objective of understanding each other's position more sympathetically, of identifying the areas of agreement and disagreement and of trying to build mutual trust so as to co-ordinate our response to threats and challenges that beset humanity today. Instead of merely talking about each other, we have tried to talk to each other, however haltingly. That is why we, instead of producing an impersonal collection of scholarly papers, have tried to collect around one table a few distinguished religious leaders of the two faiths and invite them to face each other as much as face the real issues that confront them. The fruits of this lively encounter are presented in this special issue on Christian Mission and Islamic Da'wah.

It is our considered opinion that the right approach in Christian-Muslim dialogue is to face the problems and issues that unite or divide us. These issues are legion: religious, theological, historical, socio-cultural, political. As mission/da'wah represents the outreach of one's religious tradition to the other and as the role of Christian missions in the Muslim world is regarded by the Muslims to be at the root of estrangement between the Christian and the Muslim worlds, the conference on mission and da'wah provided a natural point of departure for a meaningful dialogue.

Although there have been moments of stress and strain, expressions of human weakness and pugnacity, even wars and political encounters, Christians and Muslims have lived side by side in the Muslim world, on the whole, in peace and harmony with each other, ever since the final revelation of Islam in the seventh century.

But with the arrival of the Christian missionaries in the company of European colonizers, a new chapter began in Muslim-Christian relationships. That some of them might have been motivated by the best of spiritual intentions is not among the points in dispute. But the overall Muslim experience of the Christian mission was such that it failed to commend itself as something noble and holy. Any dispassionate evaluation of the experience would suggest that what has been achieved is a loss for Islam and religion as such, and not a gain for Christianity — the real beneficiaries being the forces of secularism, materialism and of moral insensitivity. The Muslim critique can be summed up in four points:

9

(*a*) Gross and flagrant misrepresentation of the teachings of Islam and of the life and message of the Prophet Muhammad (peace be upon him). Instead of examining Islam as it is, a totally unreal picture of Islam was concocted and used to denigrate Islam and Muslims. Although the high watermark of this type of approach to the study of Islam has passed, the effort still persists, even though in low profile and under many a disguise.

(*b*) The methodology of Christian mission concentrated upon influencing the object in a state of weakness and helplessness. Instead of direct invitation, approaches were made to those who were disadvantaged, exploiting their weaknesses for the sake of proselytism. The poor, the sick and the immature were made special targets of economic assistance, medical aid and education. Many a Christian mission acted as an organic part of colonialism and cultural imperialism. All this was a very unfair way to bring people to any religion.

(*c*) Whatever the ultimate aim, subversion of the faith and culture of Islam seems to have been the prime target of the Christian missionary enterprise. Nationalism, secularism, modernism, socialism, even communism were fostered, supported and encouraged. While the revival of Islam and the strengthening of Islamic moral life among the Muslims were, and even now are, looked upon as anathema.

(*d*) Muslims were treated as political rivals and as such subjected to overt and covert discrimination and repression. Their just causes fail to evoke any significant moral response from the Christian world. Western Christendom's attitude towards the Palestine problem in general and towards Jerusalem in particular, for example, agonizes Muslims. Majority rule is denied to Muslims in a number of African countries. The sufferings of the Muslims in such places as Eritrea, Mindanao, Kashmir, Patani, to mention only a few, fail sufficiently to arouse the moral conscience of the Christian world. Muslims are puzzled when they compare the relative lack of Christian concern over the increasing de-Christianization of the Christian world with their obsession with what amounts to de-Islamization of the Muslim world.

This being the nature of the Muslim concern it was but natural that any meaningful dialogue must begin with a review of the Christian and Muslim positions in respect of the whole experience of mission and *da'wah*. The Conference concentrated upon two major aspects of the problem: the fundamental position of Islam and Christianity in respect of *da'wah* and mission and the Christian and Muslim experience of each other's missionary/*da'wah* activity. Both religions are light-sharing. But there are differences in the way they offer their message to others and, at a deeper level, in the way they concern themselves with the world.

The two sections on the nature and concept of the Christian mission and Islamic *da'wah* and the discussions that follow bring this into sharp focus. The missionary experience of the two communities too has its disparities. A careful perusal of the material presented here will show that three issues emerge distinctly from the debate:

First, there has been widespread abuse of Christian *diakonia* and something effective needs to be done to bring an end to that. Secondly, the whole question of secularism and Westernization has to be studied in the context of religio-historical traditions of Islam and Christianity. Greater sensitivity needs to be shown to differences in the religious ideals and the historical situations of the Christian West and the Muslim world. Thirdly, although human freedom is even more essential for the flowering of man's spiritual and religious life than for his political existence, freedom becomes meaningful only within a framework of commitments and responsibilities. As such, equal concern should be shown towards the freedom and integrity of the individual and the solidarity of the community.

With these key issues in perspective, the importance of the Conference statement becomes clear. Although representing the consensus of a few persons, its significance lies in the fact that it can show the way to a more universal consensus. Its uniqueness lies in the spirit of frankness and fairness in which it is offered. It represents an attitude of loyalty to God and not necessarily to one's "tribe"; acceptance of facts, whether pleasant or unpleasant; and respect for the viewpoint and the feelings of others. With such an approach, man can move towards a new world of mutuality and pro-existence. If this is what we are aiming at, then the Chambésy Statement could be a milestone.

What about the future? The Chambésy spirit and the concrete suggestions it frames represent a first step on a long and arduous road men of goodwill from Christianity and Islam will have to tread if they want to change Christian-Muslim relations for the better. The mini-consensus evolved at Chambésy deserves to be *widened* as well as *deepened*. It contains the seeds from which the tree of some universal consensus can grow. To deepen the consensus, efforts should be made to organize a series of conferences, seminars, conventions and colloquia at different levels with a view to developing better understanding of each others' religious and historical tradition; to frame ethical rules governing dialogue, co-operation and even healthy competition; to jointly produce works of serious scholarship and frank encounters and to participate jointly in centres and institutions devoted to serving these purposes. Along with widening and deepening the consensus, effective steps should be taken to implement the proposals contained in the statement. This is an area where organizations like the World Council of Churches, the Vatican, the Islamic Secretariat, the Muslim World League, The Call of Islam Society, the Islamic Council of Europe and the like can make some significant contribution not only in healing the wounds and clearing the debris but also in building new bridges to bring the family of Abraham closer in love and mutual trust. If the Chambésy Conference and the present efforts of the IRM, the Islamic Foundation and the Centre for the Study of Islam and Christian-Muslim Relations in Europe could make some opening in that direction, this small step could be the precursor of a great change.

KHURSHID AHMAD
The Islamic Foundation, Leicester, England

This conference on Christian Mission and Islamic *Da'wah* may well mark the first occasion in the history of Christian-Muslim relations of members of the two faiths meeting, albeit informally, to discuss an area of commitment which is fundamental to their respective faiths; for *da'wah* is to Islam as mission is to Christianity, and of the latter Dr Samartha has written in an earlier issue of this journal, "to reject mission is to take out the oil of the lamp". The issue of mission and *da'wah* has of course arisen in earlier meetings between Muslims and Christians, and some of the implications for practical relationships have been recognized and commended for further discussion. But never before, to my knowledge, have Christians and Muslims met together at an international level to address themselves explicitly to this vital issue which is elemental to the integrity of both.

This fact in itself makes the conference one of significance, whatever conclusions individuals may draw from reading the record of proceedings in the pages following. The CWME and IRM are to be congratulated for the boldness of their initiative in calling the conference into being, and I know I speak for all the participants in expressing thanks for the depth of concern shown, and the warmth of hospitality extended by those responsible.

The absolute commitment of the Christian to mission and of the Muslim to *da'wah* has undoubtedly been one of the principal contributory factors to the tension, and at times conflict, which has so extensively characterized the relationship between Christianity and Islam. Each feels itself to have been abused by the other, though not necessarily in the same way, and the pains of grievance continue to this day, with Muslims — I believe with justification — incensed to the point of outrage by certain aspects of Christian action in the name of mission. To this the following pages bear ample witness. Some Christian participants in the discussions, amongst whom I include myself, may have felt that Muslim sensitivity to the breadth of new missionary thought and action within Christianity was dulled by their very justified anger with other practices which, though older, are by no means dead. Nonetheless I urge all Christian readers to take to heart, in humility and with utter seriousness, the grievances expressed by the Muslim participants. The experience of this conference has left me convinced that however well-intentioned and well-informed Christians may be about Islam, rarely are they sufficiently sensitive to the depth and implications of the Muslim sense of injury at the hand of the Christian missionary.

The conference discussion was intense throughout, and at times emotions erupted in a manner painful to Muslims and Christians alike. Perhaps this is as it should have been in a first conference on mission and *da'wah*, which could in no way abstract itself from the burden of mistrust which besets the missionary relationship between Muslim and Christian. Certainly the Christian participants wish to record their gratitude to the Muslims for their accepting to enter into this encounter, given the fact that each Muslim participant had had, in various ways, personal experience of western Christian missionaries which had left him suspicious of Christian motives in mission and reluctant to engage in discussion with missionaries. Gratitude must also be expressed for the honesty with which the Muslims spoke — an honesty manifestly inspired by the desire for improved relations in the future.

In planning the conference it seemed desirable, in the interests of intimacy of discussion, to restrict the number of participants to six Muslims and six Christians, in addition to the two co-editors and certain WCC staff members, and to invite participants experienced in missionary encounter with people of the other faith in parts of the world where Islam and Christianity are in daily contact. A list of the participants follows these editorial comments.

Unfortunately not all who had been invited were, in the event, able to attend. The absence of Professor Ishtiaq Qureshi, formerly Vice-Chancellor of the University of Karachi, Pakistan, was deeply regretted. An Islamic scholar and spokesman of such repute, and one so well read in Christianity, with long personal experience of Christian missionwork, would certainly have brought valuable perspectives to the discussion, but of this benefit the conference was deprived through insoluble technical difficulties.

The inability, at the eleventh hour, of Dr Subhi Saleh and Metropolitan Georges Khodre to travel from Beirut was a further sorely-felt loss to the conference. The agony of the present protracted conflict between Christians and Muslims in Lebanon was amongst the considerations which made the calling of a conference such as this urgent. And it was precisely because the shadow of Lebanese events haunted with such chill the consciences of all, that the conference ached from the absence of a Lebanese voice, and particularly the voices of the two Lebanese we had wanted to hear.

Discussion throughout the first half of the conference centred around formal papers commissioned from several Christian and Muslim participants, and circulated to all participants in advance. These papers, in which the writers presented their personal understandings of Christian Mission and Islamic *Da'wah*, and also certain case studies of Muslim experience of mission and Christian experience of *da'wah* (with attention to both the historical and the contemporary), are here published in the order in which they were given. To each paper a Muslim and a Christian participant were invited to respond in prelude to a "round-the-table" discussion in which the issues were developed in such ways as participants felt most fruitful, under the guidance of the chair which was held by different participants in turn. The latter part of the conference was given to a consideration of ways whereby Christians and Muslims could seek to improve their practical relationship while at the same time retaining their imperative commitments to mission and *da'wah*. This led, if somewhat hesitantly, to the preparation of a final document which is generally expressive of the concerns and hopes of the participants, though some would not wish it to be read as a statement of their personal views on all subjects mentioned, of which certain received little if any discussion round the table. All the discussion was recorded and is available on tapes, from which the coeditors subsequently extracted and edited a sequence of excerpts which, in their opinion, contain the most interesting material for a general readership.

The co-editors humbly offer their work in the succeeding pages, with all its imperfections, in the belief that the participants in the discussions in Chambésy have contributed in a small but significant way to the cause of greater understanding between two great missionary faiths. One could have wished for better results, the fruit of a more searching, questing, mutually-relating enterprise of partly-common, always loyal minds. But, what we have raises many issues for our future consideration, and may cause us to question inherited assumptions about mission and *da'wah*.

This conference has taught me much which I believe to be important in dialogue between men of living faiths; notably, that if our commitment to "togetherness" is persistent, this itself can contain the sharp and at times angry controversy of inter-religious debate, which may then be turned to productive result. This conference must lay once and for all the suspicion of the skeptic that dialogue is a passing of courtesies; it never has been, and after this conference it never will be. Furthermore, I believe the conference brings sharply before the attention of Christians the need to reflect with greater clarity upon the proper relationship between mission and dialogue, in recognition that we are living in a situation not simply of plurality of religions, but of plurality of missions. How we cope with this situation, at once critically and openly, is an issue which calls urgently for the consideration of missiologist and missionary alike.

In conclusion I would thank, with deep gratitude of a friendship matured through experiences such as here recorded, my co-editor, Brother Khurshid, whose resources of energy are matched only by his patient disposition toward his younger colleague.

DAVID KERR.

Centre for the Study
of Islam and
Christian-Muslim Relations

Selly Oak Colleges
Birmingham, England

PARTICIPANTS

Mr Khurshid Ahmad is Director General of the Islamic Foundation, Leicester.

Bishop Kenneth Cragg lectures in the University of Sussex, England, and is Episcopal Assistant Bishop in Jerusalem and the Middle East.

Dr Isma'il R. al-Faruqi is Professor of Islamic Studies, Temple University, Philadelphia.

Father Michael Fitzgerald is Director of the Pontificio Istituto di Studi Arabi in Rome.

Professor Joseph Hajjar, a Greek-Catholic expert in Canon Law and Church History, with specialization in the history of Muslim-Christian relations in the Near East, teaches in Damascus, Syria.

Professor Ihromi is Rector of Sekolah Tinggi Theologia, Jakarta, Indonesia.

Mr A. Irfan is Editor of *Impact International*, London.

Dr David Kerr is Lecturer in Islamics, Selly Oak Colleges, Birmingham, and Director of the Centre for the Study of Islam and Christian-Muslim Relations.

Mr Ali Muhsin Barwani, former Deputy Prime Minister and Minister for External Affairs in the Government of Zanzibar, Leader of the Zanzibar Nationalist Party and editor of the *Mwongozim*, a weekly paper, now lives in Cairo.

Dr Ishtiaq Quraishi, of the University of Karachi, was at the last minute unable to attend the consultation.

Dr Muhammed Rasjidi, former Minister of Religious Affairs of the Government of Indonesia, is presently Professor of Islamic Studies, University of Indonesia, Jakarta.

Bishop Arne Rudvin, Bishop of the United Church of Pakistan, lives in Karachi.

Dr Subhi Saleh, Vice-Mufti of Lebanon, was at the last minute unable to attend the consultation.

Dr Lamin Sanneh is Lecturer in the Department of Religious Studies, University of Legon, Ghana, and Research Advisor to the Islam in Africa Project.

OBSERVERS

The Rev. Emilio Castro is Director of the Commission on World Mission and Evangelism of the WCC and Editor of the *International Review of Mission*.

Dr John Taylor is Associate for Christian-Muslim Relations in the programme for Dialogue with People of Living Faiths and Ideologies, WCC.

THE CONCEPT AND PRACTICE OF CHRISTIAN MISSION

ARNE RUDVIN

Bishop of Karachi, United Church of Pakistan

I have been asked to present an introductory paper on the concept and practice of Christian mission, based upon scriptural and theological sources, and in relationship to Islam. I propose to address myself to two questions: What is the true nature of Christian mission? What is the motive of Christian mission? ...or to put it very simply: Why mission?

The practice of mission raises the question: what form should Christian mission take? In answering this question I propose to deal not with the history of mission, but rather to set out some thoughts about what the form of Christian mission should be in principle, and how Christian mission should, in principle, be undertaken. The question of "how mission?" is of course closely related to the question "why mission?"

The search for answers to these questions in this paper will be based upon the New Testament and upon Christian theological sources. By the latter I understand the theological motives underlying the Scriptural command to evangelization, and the Church's ecumenical thinking about Christ as expressed in the confessions of the Church based upon the Scriptures rather than on the ideas of any particular Christian theologian. Our attention is drawn to Christological questions regarding the incarnation, since these underlie the whole idea of mission in the New Testament.

I. The "Why" of Mission

For evangelical Christians the question of the "why" of mission does not appear to raise any problems. Mission is seen as the personal duty of every individual Christian, who is called as part of his or her faith to witness and to evangelize. The evidence is found in Scripture, and notably in the concluding verses of the Gospel of St Matthew which constitute the Great Commission:

> Go, therefore, make disciples of all the nations; baptize them in the name of th Father and of the Son and of the Holy Spirit (Matt. 28 : 19).[1]

But is there in fact any clear commandment in the New Testament to the effect that every individual Christian has a duty to witness and to preach the Gospel? The answer depends on how we read the Scriptures. If, on the one

---

[1] All biblical quotations in this article, unless otherwise indicated, are from the Jerusalem Bible.

hand, we read the New Testament as a collection of divinely inspired principles and commandments, everything being applied in exact detail to every Christian, our answer to the above question must be affirmative. But if we read the New Testament in its historical context and ask to whom specific verses were addressed, I would argue that there is then no general commandment to every Christian to preach or to witness in word to the Gospel in his or her individual capacity.

However, let us put the question differently: Has Christ given the apostolate of mission to his Church in general, or has he given it only to the twelve apostles and other apostles and members of the Church as part of their special ministries? Here the answer from Scripture is clear and unambiguous. All the writings of the New Testament are either direct missionary literature or written in a missionary situation. Each of the four Gospels can be said to prepare the way for Pentecost, the founding of the Church, through the evangelistic preaching of the apostles. The "Acts of the Apostles" is the first history of mission, and at the same time it is the first history of the Church. In the New Testament the history of the Church and the history of mission are one and the same, and this remained so for several hundreds of years of subsequent Christian history.

All the New Testament Gospels are to be classed as missionary literature and they all lead up to the commandment to evangelize. Therefore any understanding of the nature of the apostolate of mission as it continues in the Church must begin with the Gospels, and we should pay close attention to them:

Matthew 28 : 18-19

> All authority in heaven and on earth has been given to me. Go therefore, make disciples of all the nations; baptize them in the name of the Father and of the Son and of the Holy Spirit.

Mark 16 : 15-16

> Go out to the whole world; proclaim the Good News to all creation. He who believes and is baptized will be saved; he who does not believe will be condemned.

Luke 24 : 47-48

> In his name, repentance for the forgiveness of sins would be preached to all the nations, beginning from Jerusalem. You are witnesses to this.

John 20 : 21-23

> "As the Father sent me, so am I sending you." After saying this he breathed on them and said: "Receive the Holy Spirit. For those whose sins you forgive, they are forgiven; for those whose sins you retain, they are retained."

John 20 : 31

> These are recorded so that you may believe that Jesus is the Christ, the son of God, and that believing this you may have life through his name.

Cf. Acts 1 : 8

> But you will receive power when the Holy Spirit comes on you, and then you will be my witnesses not only in Jerusalem but throughout Judaea, and Samaria and indeed to the ends of the earth.

Clearly the command to proclaim the Gospel and to make disciples extends to all nations, to the ends of the world, to the whole creation; there can be no limitation, for the Gospel is for all people. The same conviction is to be found in the letters of St Paul and also of St Peter, who understood the Gospel as meant not only for the Jews who already had the law, but also for all the Gentiles. In this there is also a deeper theological meaning, that through the Gospel the enmity and divisions between Jews and Gentiles shall be broken down. They shall be reconciled to each other through their participation in Christ's love; they shall become not only brethren but a single family, members of the same body of Christ: "it means that pagans now share the same inheritance, that they are parts of the same body, and that the same promise has been made to them, in Christ Jesus, through the Gospel." (Eph. 3 : 6.)

Earlier Protestant missions had as their main motivation and purpose that individuals should be saved through faith in Jesus Christ and this is undoubtedly in accordance with the New Testament as shown in the passages quoted above : "Those who are baptized will be saved" (Mark); "repentance for the forgiveness of sins" (Luke); "the authority to forgive sins given to the apostles" (John). Peter, in his great mission speech, recorded in the Acts of the Apostles, says: "for all the names in the world given to men, this is the only one by which we can be saved." (Acts 4 : 12.)

Some may feel this call to personal salvation to be too anthropocentric a motivation for mission today; indeed there are Christians who may feel embarrassed by this type of thinking, but no-one can deny that it is a fundamental scriptural reason for the "why" of mission.

It may be correct to balance this call to individual repentance with the more positive assertion that there *is salvation in Jesus Christ*. But there is a yet more positive, or Christocentric, assertion which finds powerful expression in the New Testament, namely that we are saved in order to belong to Christ. This means that we are baptized in Christ's name not only to receive forgiveness of our sins and to be saved, but in order that we shall belong to Jesus Christ who is now the Lord of everything and everybody. We are baptized into his body, into the Church of which he is the head. This idea is intrinsic to the great commission to mission as we have seen it in the Gospels, where the main motivation for making disciples is that "all authority in heaven and on earth has been given to me" (Matt. 28 : 18). This is the main idea in Paul's letter to the Philippians (2 : 9-11) where he writes: "But God raised him high and gave him the name which is above all other names so that all beings in the heavens, on earth and in the underworld, should bend the knee at the name of Jesus and that every tongue should acclaim Jesus Christ as Lord to the glory of God the Father."

Compare also the letter to the Ephesians (1 : 20-23), which recalls the mighty works which God accomplished ". . . in Christ, when he raised him from the dead and made him sit at his right hand, in heaven, far above every Sovereignty, Authority, Power or Domination, or any other name that can be named, not only in this age but also in the age to come. He has put all things under his feet, and made him, as the ruler of everything, the head of the Church, which is his body, the fullness of him who fills the whole creation."

So the faith of the New Testament is that Jesus is Lord, and that everything and everybody rightly belongs to him. Mission, therefore, is to bring all mankind to acknowledge Jesus as Lord, because he owns us all, and has a just claim on us all. Here we have the real motivation for mission. It follows, therefore, that a proper Christian theology of mission depends on our Christology; mission in the New Testament is only a corollary of what the New Testament writers assert about Christ, and perhaps much of the weaknesses and confusion in modern Christian mission thinking are due either to the fact that we treat missiology separately from Christology, or to the confusion and uncertainty in our Christology; perhaps our Christology is not closely enough related to the incarnation of God the Son.

For the apostolate to Islam it is quite clear that this is the crucial point. The Lordship of Jesus in the absolute sense is contested by Islam and thereby the very foundation and motive for Christian mission to Islam is questioned. This means that one of the most important by-products of the Christian apostolate to the Muslim world will be to force the Christian Church to take its Christology absolutely seriously in all its aspects. I personally am convinced that if we want to have an honest meeting with Islam, and an honest discussion here in our seminar, we will have to apply ourselves diligently to the Christological question. The incarnation does not primarily mean that in Jesus Christ we have real humanity, though that is, of course true, but that in Jesus Christ we have God who *really* became man.

This is the main issue we have to face, and it would be disaster to avoid it through a watered-down Christology more or less over-shadowed by theories about natural revelation. This is an absolute must if we want to have honest dialogue. The real motive in the New Testament for mission is that the crucified and risen Jesus is Lord. This is substantially more than saying that Jesus gives us a saving knowledge, or that he reveals something from God; in either case it could be rightly argued that this knowledge and revelation may be found in other places, better or poorer, twisted or perverted, usually judged according to the degree of our own intolerance.

The real New Testament motivation for mission is that Jesus Christ, himself, is God revealed: "He who has seen me has seen the Father." (John 14 : 9 RSV.) He, himself, is salvation and eternal life: "I am the Way, the Truth and the Life." (John 14 : 6.) "The Truth" should perhaps be translated into the Islamic context as *al-Haqq*. Jesus is Lord through whom everything is created and one day everyone shall acknowledge him as Lord (Phil. 2 : 10, 11; Eph. 1 : 23). The Lord is here taken in the absolute sense and should perhaps be translated into the Islamic context as *Rabb al-'Ālamīn*.

19

In the post-resurrection New Testament, "Lord" means "God" and this we can clearly see in the Gospel according to St John where the climax of the whole gospel is in the confession of Thomas, "My Lord and my God", and we see that every attribute connected with the Lord of the Old Testament can be attributed to Jesus Christ in the New Testament.[2] This is the faith and confession of the New Testament and the real motivation for its mission and answers our question about the "why" of Christian mission.

If it is not understood that this is the motivation for the mission of the Christian Church, then mission will be considered only as an expression of the intolerance and fanaticism of the Church, or as an expression of the colonialism of the Western world in the religious field. The reason why the WCC is engaged in the world-wide mission is that it consists of "Churches which confess the Lord Jesus Christ as God and Saviour according to the Scriptures". The phrase "God and Saviour" indicates the deepest motivation for Christian mission. God has become man in order to be our Saviour; God in his love for us gave himself for us (II Cor. 5 : 14-21); God was in Christ and became sin for our sake; his love compels us to preach the good news about salvation in him in order that he may be acknowledged as Lord and Saviour by every man; we as his Church no longer belong to ourselves but to him.

The motive for mission that emphasizes that each individual man must be saved, and that which says that all men must belong to him at this point converge. We were created and he came in order that we may become members of his body and his Church of which he is the head. (Eph. 1 : 4-23 "... that God would bring everything together under Christ, as head, everything in the heavens and everything on earth ... He has put all things under his feet, and made him as the ruler of everything, the head of the Church, which is his body, the fullness of him who fills the whole creation.")

The Church is not a group of people who think more or less the same way or have a common interest. Rather the Church exists in God's will from before the creation of the world and we are baptized into it, not only in order that we may receive the forgiveness of our sins and be saved, but that we shall be made members of Christ's Body, to whom we rightly belong because he has a claim upon us all. This does not mean that we are baptized in order simply that the Church will have some more members, but that his body may be completed. The existence of his Church, his body on earth means that the kingdom of heaven is here, that *jannah* is here; that salvation is in the world here and now and available to men by faith in Jesus Christ. "And eternal life is this: to know you, the only true God, and Jesus Christ whom you have sent." (John 17 : 3.)

It is one of the motives for mission that his body may be completed; but the corollary is that the role and purpose of the Church in this world is — and must be — to proclaim the love of God given to us in Christ our Lord, that there

---

[2] See Oscar Cullman: *The Christology of the New Testament* (1973).

is salvation in him, and that he is our Lord. But her task is also to implement in her life the new commandment that we shall love each other as he has loved us (John 13 : 34-35) — love which should also reach out to those who have not yet become members of his body as he loved us and gave himself for us when we were enemies and strangers.

II. The "How" of Mission

We must now address ourselves to the second of our two questions: what form should Christian mission take? How should Christians practise mission? One of the most taxing issues in Christian missionary thinking today seems to be: what is the proper relationship between the proclamation of the good news of the Gospel and Christian service, or *diakonia* as it is termed in the Greek of the New Testament, meaning to live out the Gospel in selfless service and social action for others who are in need and trouble.

In the New Testament it seems that the task of mission is overwhelmingly thought of as being the commission to proclaim the good news — evangelization. The apostles were witnesses of the life of Jesus, his crucifixion and resurrection, and concerning these they were called to be witnesses before all people so that all may believe. In relation to this central theme, the New Testament seems to place *diakonia* — service extended to those in need — in a secondary position, and certainly more in the background than is the case with much modern missionary thought. For this change of emphasis, I would suggest, there seem to be two reasons, one theological and the other practical.

The practical reason is the result of the changed economic situation of most of the Christian world. In the early Church, the Gospel was brought from a poor country, Palestine, to the more prosperous regions of Asia Minor and Greece, and as a result we find that the daughter churches were sending gifts — "aid", as we would say — to Jerusalem, to the mother Church which remained beset by economic difficulties. Today the situation is reversed. The countries in which the Church is numerically strong and established happens to be the richer "developed" countries and the younger churches belong to a great extent to "developing" countries, and this has had a marked effect on the practical shape of mission. Besides the political and other problems to which this situation gives rise, it has made the question of the relationship between the proclamation of the Gospel and *diakonia* a burning issue. How can we preach to starving or sick people without first helping them materially if it is in our power to do so. The New Testament itself forces such questions on us when we read such words as these of Jesus, "I have not come to be served but to serve"; and we are reminded in the first letter of John (3 : 16-17), "This has taught us love — that he gave up his life for us; and we, too, ought to give up our lives for our brothers. If a man who was rich enough in this world's goods saw that one of his brothers was in need, but closed his heart to him, how could the love of God be living in him."

According to Luke, writing in the Acts of the Apostles, the first office to be separated from the apostolate was that of deacon, which was to be responsible for looking after the needy in the congregation. But this decision was reached, as Acts 6 makes clear, in order to ensure that the apostles could concentrate fully on their activity of preaching:

> ... there were murmurings ... because the widows were neglected in the daily distribution. And the twelve disciples summoned the body of disciples and said: "It is not right that we should give up preaching the word of God to serve tables. Therefore, brothers, pick out from among you seven men of good repute, full of the Spirit and wisdom, whom we may appoint to this duty. But we will devote ourselves to prayer and to the ministry of the word" (Acts 6 : 1-4, RSV).

Preaching, clearly, was seen as the first duty of the apostles, and as a matter of principle the practice of the *diakonia*, or service, was considered to be the fruit of the Gospel.

Diakonia is not mission "proper" but the true fruit of the preaching of the Gospel about him who gave himself for us and who came to serve rather than to be served. But the *diakonia* should not be thought of simply as *a* fruit but *the* fruit of the Gospel. The whole Gospel is a witness to God's self-sacrificing love in Christ and the purpose of the preaching of the Gospel is that Christians should be able to live in his *agapé* (love) and serve all who are in need, whether it be physically or spiritually.

But the Gospel proper remains the good news that he loved us first and that therefore we must love each other. But while our love is always to be understood as a fruit or a gift of the Spirit given when we believe in the Gospel, springing out of our thankfulness to him, we always practise it imperfectly and mix it with all sorts of other motives. When we analyse the fruit in our lives empirically and psychologically, I wonder whether it would not be more correct to call it "slag products" than "fruit". At the best it is an indication that Christ touched us with his love, but it is also an indication that he has met us in all our weaknesses, sins and impurities. It follows, however, that the fruit, if such it may be called, cannot itself create faith or give men new life, for it is the pure Word of God who alone is able to create faith. And Christians should never forget this as they practise their mission: their missionary responsibility is to preach, and our only motive in *diakonia* should be, as an expression of love, to assist the needy person because he is in need.

In the New Testament, *diakonia* always has its natural beginning in the Church amongst the believers, but it is never limited to them; they provide the beginning but not the end. This seems now and then to be forgotten in modern mission, where we find a certain tendency to institutionalize and internationalize Christian service. This raises the question as to how far institutionalized *diakonia* may be considered a living expression of faith. Beside the temptation to make these institutions instruments of proselytization, such institutionalization may also result in the local church and congregations becoming divorced from Christian service, and therefore becoming passive and introspective. It is my opinion that we have, in modern missionary practice, too often succumbed to the temptation to make these institutions means of influence or of evangelization ; I believe our Muslim brethren have a right to blame us for this; dependence upon these as means of evangelization is also a sign that we lack faith in the Word of God and in the power of his Spirit.

When mission institutions have been used in this way, they degrade medical, educational and Christian service in general: these institutions are fully justified in themselves by the very existence of the need which they meet. If we have any ulterior motive for our service, however good, *diakonia* is no longer an expression of *agapé* but becomes a propaganda instrument.

When the Church confesses the crucified and risen Jesus to be God and Saviour, it confesses the faith of the New Testament that God is what the self-sacrificing, serving love we see in Jesus of Nazareth declares Him to be: *agapé*. The very essence of God upon which his divinity rests is *agapé* (I John 4 : 8-10) and therefore the Church does not feel it to be impossible that God the Son in his love suffers for us. And if *agapé* really is his essence, then God is completely and fully revealed for us only on the Cross. If we fail to perceive this, then the incarnation and crucifixion remain only a scandal or foolishness.

From this it follows that the purpose and meaning of the life of the Church is to live in his love and to try to live it out in service in the Church and outside. To be compelled by his love is therefore empirically the gift of salvation — saved from self-centredness and self-consciousness. To serve those who are in need of service is therefore a necessary activity within the life of the Church, but it should not be misused as an instrument of influence or propaganda, and thus be degraded. Therefore, we should welcome the new trend where Churches, organizations and mission agencies are taking part in social/economic programmes without any evangelistic purpose or intention. My only concern is that the local churches should be drawn into this, not only with personnel but also with locally-raised funds. The undertaking of such work together with non-Christian bodies is also a development which should be welcomed.

When we remember the affluence of most of the so-called Christian countries, we should pray and work for a much greater involvement in all sorts of economic and social projects in the suffering world. However, my personal conviction is that the word "mission" should not be used in this connection, for there is, as I have argued from the New Testament, a proper scriptural distinction between evangelism and service.

In this connection it is important that we do not forget the eschatological aspects of the New Testament. The Church is not here to save the world nor to remain in the world forever. The Church is in the world and is called to serve the world but she is not of the world. The Church is a people walking towards a goal, looking forward to Christ's coming again. This can so easily be ignored in our eagerness to serve and improve man's situation here and now. Such eagerness is entirely proper, provided always that we remember that the real Gospel is not development or progress but the proclamation that He loved us first and that we only attain real life through faith in the crucified and risen Lord.

What, then, should we say in positive terms about the practice of mission? What form should mission take in principle? The New Testament is quite clear that it should be the proclamation of the good news about what God the Father has done for us in Jesus Christ. The proclamation of the good news in Jesus through preaching to all men (and the giving of its fruits in the sacraments) is the instrument by which the Holy Spirit creates faith. As we read in Paul's letter to the Romans (10 : 14, KJ): "How then shall they call on him in whom they have not believed? and how shall they believe in him whom they have not heard? and how shall they hear without a preacher?" The apostolate to preach, the proclamation of the good news about Christ, is given to the Church not only for formal preaching but that the whole life of the Church should be a witness to the love of God as it meets us in Jesus Christ. As a reaction against the too narrow definition of preaching in some Protestant mission circles, we are today inclined to stress that the whole life of the Church should be a witness to Christ, including its liturgical life, *diakonia*, and all the many different ways by which the life of the Church is expressed in and to the world. But if we are to take the New Testament as the normative source regarding the practice and form of mission, we cannot escape the fact that the proclamation of the Gospel is seen to be the main expression of the apostolate of mission.

The main task of the twelve disciples and of the other apostles (Barnabas, Paul, etc.) was to evangelize. The very meaning of this word is to proclaim the Good News. The content of the message is handed over to the evangelist. He does not primarily present his own experience, although he may want to share it, but is commissioned to deliver a message. The main task of the twelve was to proclaim the *kerygma* or preaching about Christ. "The apostle", it has rightly been said, "does not have any personal influence on the inner form of his commission".

The characteristic mark of the office of the twelve disciples and the apostles was that they were evangelists, called to deliver a message. It goes without saying that they believe absolutely in the message, and they themselves witness that it is truth and life, but they do not have any influence over its content; that is given. The content is Jesus, his incarnation, his suffering, his death and resurrection. Moreover the interpretation of the meaning of the message was given to the original apostles as a gift from the Lord himself, through the Holy Spirit. They were not free to change the interpretation according to the circumstances. The Gospel is the proclamation of what happened in Jesus Christ and what the real meaning of this happening is and what its consequences are for mankind. The content of the Gospel is not open for discussion. The official evangelization by the Church must be, in principle and practice, the proclamation of a certain given message. This would seem, in my opinion, at least, to exclude dialogue as a proper form of evangelization and therefore of mission. What individual Christians may do in their private capacity is a different thing. Dialogue, together with the modesty and respect for other religious experiences which dialogue properly implies, may here have a rightful place. Everyone with some knowledge and experience of the piety and the expression of religious experience in non-Christian religions, in our case Islam, will of course admit that they are subjectively as good as anything in Christian piety and experience, and we as Christians must respect them as much (or as little) as we respect our own piety and experience. Some of us, indeed, may doubt if our own piety and experience as such is really worth sharing, but while it may be very right to be modest in this regard, the evangelist, as herald, is not called to be modest on behalf of his Lord or on behalf of the Gospel.

A quite different issue is that the Gospel we are called to proclaim is to be translated not only into different languages, but also into different cultures, different thought patterns and different religious worlds. Here dialogue is definitely necessary for practical and hermeneutic reasons — in order that we can be sure that the listener understands anything at all. Often the evangelist may feel that everything he says is understood in quite a different way from that which he intends. Paradoxically, this may especially be true in the case of Islam, because there are many religious ideas, terms and structures which seem so similar whereas in fact their specific meanings and context are often quite different from those of the Christian.

Here we face what I regard as the major practical theological difficulty in the Christian apostolate to Islam, and I believe that the *da'wah* of Islam to Christians in some way must meet the same problem. In this context dialogue might prove to be a practical necessity for both parties. But on the other hand, it should be clear that Jesus Christ has commissioned his Church to proclaim a message given by him and we are not at liberty to change this message as it may be deemed necessary or expedient in the dialogue situation.

We do not enter dialogue with an open mandate to modify the message we bring if need may arise. Christians are bound, today as always in the past, by their obedience to the apostolic witness to Christ as recorded in the Scriptures. As the content of the Gospel is given, according to the New Testament, we may also say that in principle the form is given. It is proclamation and more specifically proclamation which has the form of a promise. This is especially clear in the writings of St Paul as evidenced particularly in the fourth chapter of his letter to the Romans. The Gospel is not our word but God's own creative Word, because it has a promise for those who hear that he will save them through that which has been achieved in Christ.

The apostle or evangelist, indeed any preacher, has not only to preach the good news of Jesus Christ, but as part of the good news which he preaches to proclaim God's promise of absolution. It is this which invests the preaching with God's own authority, and where the promise is absent the preaching is reduced to words about God and it is no longer God's own Word. And precisely because the evangelism contains both proclamation and promise, the Holy Spirit can use this word to create faith. In the end it is God himself who speaks, in the proclamation of the Good News, and it is this which we in a Christian sense call the "Word of God", of which the Scripture is a trustworthy record and Canon by which we judge.

He who commissioned the apostles is still the head of the Church, living and present with us where the word is preached and the sacraments administered, where two or three are gathered together in his name. In certain practical situations this may outwardly take the form of dialogue but in principle it is something quite different. It is God himself addressing sinful man with a word of forgiveness, a promise, a word of life to one who is dead.

It is through this promise, God's own Word to me, that the Holy Spirit creates faith. Faith is God's free gift of grace and not something which is the result of argument, persuasion or propaganda. Therefore the Church should not use any means other than proclamation for its evangelization. Man does not in himself have power to believe or to trust that in God's grace and mercy his sins are forgiven here and now, and that God is his merciful Father in Jesus Christ.

The use of any external means to proselytize only shows a false confidence in man and a lack of faith in God's Word. It is God himself who, through his own Word, God the Son, can alone reveal God. And it is God himself who can alone perceive God; God can only be perceived through God the Holy Spirit, and therefore faith is entirely dependent on the free gift of the Spirit. The issue of natural revelation — whether there can be any knowledge, true or perverse, about God outside Jesus Christ — is in the end irrelevant, for it is a quite different kind of knowledge of God about which the New Testament speaks.

In conclusion let us return to the first question discussed in this paper: Is there anywhere in the New Testament where every individual Christian is expected to witness to and confess Jesus Christ? It seems that the earliest Christian confession "Jesus is Kurios, Jesus is Lord" (I Cor. 12 : 3) was the confession which every Christian who had received the Holy Spirit was expected to make in time of persecution, as Oscar Cullman has shown us in his *The Christology of the New Testament*.

It is only in the power of the Holy Spirit that Christian can confess Jesus to be Lord. "Lord" must here be understood with the same meaning as in the confession of Thomas referred to above, "Lord God". And this remains the confession of all the Churches, and the very purpose of their mission both in concept and practice: to confess the Lord Jesus Christ as God and Saviour according to the Apostolic witness as recorded in the Scriptures.

Dr al-Faruqi initiated discussion upon Bishop Rudvin's paper with the following points: (Editors)

al-Faruqi: The basic difficulty with Bishop Rudvin's paper is that it oscillates between being a historical statement and a statement of his personal faith. It commits the error of taking Matthew 28 : 14 as the historical evidence for the origin of the missionary command. Biblical criticism has shown that this verse belongs to a later stage of Christian development and could not have been said by Jesus. Equally, although baptism was known in those days, it was not institutionalized as a Christian sacrament in Jesus' time; nor had the "trinity" then become integral to Christian doctrine. On the other hand, the paper's claim that since the content of the Gospel has been given and since mission is dependent upon the Gospel, neither is open to discussion, strikes me as contradictory to the historical standpoint altogether. Such statements of personal faith cannot serve as basis for discussion in this conference convened precisely in order to discuss mission, Christian as well as Muslim.

Bishop Rudvin's claim that Jesus' "mission" was addressed to all men runs counter to Jesus' own statement as reported by the same authority (viz. Matthew) that he was sent only to the lost tribes of Israel. He also underrates the reformatory character of Jesus' mission, namely, to combat the specific issues of ethnocentrism and legalistic externalization of religion which had arisen among the Jews. Jesus spoke to an acute problem among his own people. This is not to deny that Jesus' mission later led to a universalist stand by Christians in consequence of his spiritualizing, internalizing and personalizing call. But his objective was to break Jewish aberration.

Instead of a paper on the nature of mission, the Bishop has given us a paper on Christology, which is not the subject of this conference. Abuse of the missionary's vocation is discussable without reference to the doctrinal content of his preaching. The missionary stands here indicted with moral and political abuses of his vocation, which are condemnable whatever the religious doctrine in whose name he claims to preach. If Christian mission to Muslims has helped to reopen the old Christological question thought to be settled once for all by the Council of Nicaea, Muslims welcome the development.

If the Christological question is to be raised at this conference, this necessarily implies reconsidering all the christologies of the ante-Nicene fathers as well as that of Islam as standing on a par with that of catholic Christianity. No discussion of the Christological question will be beneficial if one Christology is to be raised above the rest and made arbiter of all.

However, questions of methodology have to be raised and agreed upon before any christological matter is discussed. I would suggest that Christians wishing to enter into dialogue with Muslims eschew the "personal", "experiential" basis on which the Bishop based religious knowledge as epistemologically precarious. Any prejudice or hallucination can then masquerade as "religion" and claim authority on that basis.

All the arguments which the Bishop gave in support of his Christology strike me as those of a mind not acquainted with the poetical bent of the Semitic mind which belonged to Jesus as well as his disciples. Statements such as "I am the truth, the way, the life", "I and my Father are one", "Whoever has seen me has seen the Father", "lord and master", which can be repeated today by any mystic; the plural form "We" of Genesis which is still an agreeable convention of politeness — all these are common in Semitic parlance where they do not at all mean what Christians take them to mean. Like the ancient Hellenes', the Western mind does not seem to have the capacity to take Semitic anthropomorphisms, figures of speech, allegories and the like, poetically. The Semitic notion of transcendence was lost to the Christian tradition because transcendent truth can be expressed only in poetical language.

There is the even more serious side of religious and moral content. The claim that Jesus is God is the consequence of two assumptions: first, that all mankind is necessarily and hopelessly fallen (the "peccatist" thesis); and second, that God has saved them by suffering death as price of their fallenness (the "saviorist" thesis). The first is a warped view of human nature which is always as capable of doing the good as the evil. It is a non-empirical, psychopathic view of history. The second, by its emphasis on vicarious suffering, is repugnant to moral sense and cognition and destroys God's transcendence, the divine ultimacy, on the metaphysical and axiological levels. It denigrates man, flouts his moral responsibility, and renders not only *diakonia*, but religion itself, meaningless.

The separation of *kerygma* (proclamation) from *diakonia* (service) is welcome. But this elevation of *diakonia* to the place of first Christian duty is unacceptable, and precisely for the reasons Bishop Rudvin has given.

Rudvin: Several of your comments are addressed to the main point of my paper, and I must reaffirm the fact that the central proclamation of the good news of the Gospel is that Jesus is Lord, for which the Gospel in Greek used the word *kurios*. Now the early Church used the word *kurios* of Jesus in the same way as the Jews used *aduni* (Lord) in place of the holy name of God, *yaweh*, in the Hebrew of the Old Testament. In this way the early Christians could attribute to Jesus, *kurios*, all that the Jews had attributed to *yahweh*. *Kurios* in the New Testament means nothing less than *rabb al-'ālamīn* (Lord of all Being) in the usage of the Qur'ān. The earliest confessions of faith in the New Testament are Christological rather than trinitarian, as Oscar Cullmann has shown in his study *Early Christian Confessions*, the thesis of which still stands despite criticism. Indeed, the whole New Testament is a Christological confession, summed up in the confession of Thomas recorded by John, "My Lord, my God" (Jn 20 : 28) which in Hebrew would be *yahweh elohaini*. The mission of the Church is to make real for mankind Jesus as *kurios*, in whom there is salvation and eternal life. I believe this is the only justification for mission, and without this conviction I would never have dared to try to bring the Gospel to Muslims.

al-Faruqi: But your use of the term "Lord" is loaded with ambiguity, and assigning to it your specific meaning has led to a great deal of trouble.

Rudvin: But the New Testament must be taken in the light of the Old Testament. Take, for example, St John who, in chapter 8 : 58, records Jesus as saying, "Truly I say unto you, before Abraham was, I am". Here Jesus is claiming the Divine Name "I am" precisely in the Old Testament sense. Did John corrupt it? You may think so. But if we accept the New Testament as an authentic witness, then we are bound to interpret it in the light of Old Testament meanings.

al-Faruqi: But it is precisely the identity of "scripture" which is here in question, as well as the methodology of understanding and interpreting it. Knowing that the early Christians had no "scripture" except that of Judaism, that the twenty-seven books of the New Testament we know today were not canonized by the Church as "scripture" until the third century of the Christian Era, at which time there were countless apostolic epistles and "Gospels" in circulation, how can you be sure that the "Gospel" as we have it today (27 books), and as interpreted in Lutheran theology, contains the truth about God? Are not other reports about God worthy of some scholarly scrutiny? Take the word *kurios* which you claim Jesus applied to himself with a meaning similar to the *rabb al-'ālamīn* in the Qur'ān. The meaning you give it is based upon the report by John, a century after Jesus, that a certain Thomas confessed Jesus as his Lord and God. In those days there were many people attributing divine status to all sorts of men. How can you take this as evidence that Jesus called himself God? Then you say that in addition to this so-called "evidence", you experience Jesus as the living Lord. This is a reflection upon you, as much as Thomas' confession — even if proved historically — is a reflection upon him, not Jesus. It is indeed to be regretted that we have no documents from Jesus. But this ought to make us all the more careful as to what we ascribe to him *in absentia*.

Rudvin: Let me make one thing clear. By the word "Gospel" — in Greek "*Euangelion*" — I do not mean at all what the Muslim means by "*Injīl*", and I want to clarify this point to avoid Muslims interpreting the Christian Gospel in Muslim terms. "Gospel" means "proclamation of the good news", good news about the Christ event, about Jesus in whom and through whom the Kingdom of God comes into being. The Gospel is something living, and though its proclamation has been recorded in the books of the New Testament, these are not themselves the Gospel. The Gospel is good news proclaimed to the Church, which the Church in turn proclaims, and semantically in Greek it excludes the meaning of a "Book".

Hajjar: I very much appreciate the way that Bishop Rudvin has dealt with the concept of Christian mission, although there are many other and fundamental emphases within the Christian tradition which would have to be included in order to make of it a comprehensive, ecumenical statement on the

29

"why" of mission. But given the nature of this meeting, I would have liked to have seen a more specific, more direct addressing of particular Muslim concerns. For example, there is the difficulty which Muslims experience, at the conceptual level, of appreciating why Jesus Christ is so fundamental to Christian teaching and activity, there being no point of human comparison in Islam; or again, the Muslim's difficulty of appreciating how Christians see the motive of mission in Christ's death on the cross, their view of the crucifixion as being for the salvation of all mankind. Here, again, there is no point of comparison with the Islamic understanding of either man or of "salvation". To avoid any ambiguity for the Muslims, could you elaborate the idea of redemption in mission and the significance it has for witness?

Rudvin: By salvation I mean having a personal relationship with God; God declares himself in a loving and forgiving relationship to man in Jesus Christ. Mark, for example, records how Jesus, seeing the faith of those who carried the paralytic to him, said, "My son, your sins are forgiven". The Jews responded by accusing him of blasphemy: "Who can forgive sins but God alone" (Mark 2 : 5-8). But for Mark it is clear that Jesus brings salvation, forgiveness, in this world — which is what the Kingdom of God is all about: God establishing a personal relationship with man, through the incarnation and sacrifice of Christ. And for this reason I am sympathetic towards the Orthodox idea of man being drawn into the divinity of God. All this shows that the real meaning of the nature of God is forgiving love, expressed in Greek by the word *agapé*. And this calls us away from any form of Christian religious intolerance towards the very heart of the Gospel.

al-Faruqi: Permit me to remove some ambiguity regarding the term "salvation". In its general sense, Islam does of course hold that salvation is man's deep religious need. Allah is the Saviour Who forgives man his sins and saves. In Christianity, however, "salvation" has another meaning, that is, pulling man out of the sinful predicament into which he is "fallen", by nature of his very existence on earth as man, and from which he can never extricate himself by his own effort, no matter how great or moral he be. It's true, such "salvation" does not exist in Islam's vocabulary.

Now it seems to me that the Christian claim that Jesus is God is based on two assumptions: that all mankind is necessarily and hopelessly fallen — what I call "peccatism", and that God has rescued men by paying the price for their fallenness. But if men were thus fallen, why should God have rescued them anyway? To argue that it is an expression of God's *agapé* is to argue in a circle, because his *agapé* would more logically be the consequence of his having rescued them and to argue some kind of cosmic justice is a Manichaen view. Moreover, the crucifixion, as vicarious suffering, is opposed to our moral sense.

With these issues still in the air, Dr Castro introduced a further suggestion about the "why" of mission: (Editors)

Castro: In your paper, do you show with sufficient clarity the relationship between the "why" of mission and the Christian response to the love of God in witness? When we speak to Muslims about the Gospel, should we not emphasize that we do so, as the Apostle Paul said, because the love of Christ constrains us? What about mission as the Church's expression of *agapé*, the natural consequence of the treasure of the Church's faith?

Rudvin: This is fine for the personal life of the individual Christian, but not for the evangelism of the Church. As the motive of mission I find it too individualistic, too Protestant an interpretation of the Gospel. What the Apostle was actually describing in II Corinthians 5 : 14 is the motivation of his own apostolate — being constrained by love in his divine commission. But we should not as individuals identify ourselves with Paul's apostolate; our identity is rather with the congregation in Corinth to whom Paul spoke these words.

You see, I believe we must distinguish sharply between the proclamation of the Gospel, or evangelism, and Christian service, *diakonia*. Service is a very important part of Christian life and has its justification in the needs of the people who are served. But it should never be used as an instrument of mission. There should be no persuasion in mission, and to use service persuasively as an instrument of mission not only prostitutes the service but also shows a lack of faith on the part of the missionary.

al-Faruqi: I welcome Bishop Rudvin's separation of *kerygma* and *diakonia*. But what are the criteria for *diakonia*? It must have its rules and priorities, first among which is the consent of the served. In the Muslim world I believe there is no consent for the Christian *diakonia*. And even if you want to carry the Muslim to heaven on your shoulder, you must still acknowledge his priorities — and today his spiritual and political needs are more urgent than his developmental or economic ones. And before any further Christian *diakonia* takes place in the Muslim world, there is an enormous backlog of dirt in our relationship which needs to be cleaned.

Cragg: I agree with Bishop Rudvin upon the need to separate proclamation from service and compassion, if the latter is used as any sort of inducement. The accentuating problems of human poverty — in Calcutta, for example — and the structures that are involved in this are quite clearly problems confronting national governments, far beyond the private philanthropy of missionary hospitals, Red Crescent, Red Cross, etc. But at the same time, these are all problems which should bring together men of religious faith. The issues of how to serve human need in the context of the state and different religious cultures is common territory in which religions ought to generate a quality of compassion and a sense of devotion.

Dr Sanneh turned the discussion toward the problem of trans-cultural communication: (Editors)

Sanneh: Your paper gives a moving and succinct outline of Christian faith and belief, but it throws up many questions of contemporary struggle with the Christian tradition. One of those questions, for example, is: How does the Gospel help Christians to relate meaningfully to others? The confession "Jesus is Lord" is set within a certain semantic context, but translated into different African languages, for example, it raises different ideas. And the proclaimer must face the reality that part of his message is his own personality. The creed of Christianity is bound up, to greater and lesser degree, with the biography of the proclaimers, so that the listeners have to relate to the proclaimer's context as well as to the proclamation. How should we tackle this problem?

Rudvin: I agree that the translation of the Gospel into different cultural contexts is tremendously difficult and important, and it has been throughout all Christian history from the very beginning. It's for this reason that the pure Gospel could have been lost when it was transplanted into the Greek context. How then, after that, can we surely identify the Christian Gospel? Well, I believe that Jesus was not only a man in history, at a particular time and place, but that we know him also as the risen Jesus, living inside his Church as an objective ontological reality. I believe that he is now even more incarnated than before. And we know this reality through the Holy Spirit which creates faith as a gift which is given again and again.

The way we relate the Gospel to a new cultural context, such as Africa, for example, is by the new commandment (Jn 13 : 34) which lies at the heart of the Gospel. This new commandment is not just that we should love one another — this is to be found in many other religions, including Islam. The new commandment is that we must love one another "as I have loved you" — that is to say, love our neighbour, whoever he is instead of loving ourselves, in the manner of the self-giving love of Jesus. It is just the historical fact of the Cross, which was God's own act of love, which makes it possible to translate and relate the Gospel to every cultural context. So when John talks about being in God he's not talking about mysticism, *tasawwuf* (sufism), but about *agapé* which means self-giving love for all men. And here I believe we have a tremendously important point of practical and ethical content which can lead to a co-operation with other religions at a much deeper level than that of metaphysical discussion.

32

ON THE NATURE OF ISLAMIC DA'WAH

Isma'il al-Faruqi

Professor of Islamics, Temple University, Philadelphia, USA

Allah, *subhānahu wa ta'ālā*, has commanded the Muslim: "Call men unto the path of your Lord by wisdom and goodly counsel. Present the cause to them through argument yet more sound" (Qur'ān 16 : 125). *Da'wah* is the fulfilment of this commandment "to call men unto the path of Allah." Besides, it is the effort by the Muslim to enable other men to share and benefit from the supreme vision, the religious truth, which he has appropriated. In this respect it is rationally necessary, for truth wants to be known. It exerts pressure on the knower to share his vision of it with his peers. Since religious truth is not only theoretical, but also axiological and practical, the man of religion is doubly urged to take his discovery to other men. His piety, his virtue and charity impose upon him the obligation to make common the good which has befallen him.

I. Da'wah Methodology

A. Da'wah is not coercive

"Calling" is certainly not coercing. Allah (*s.w.t.*) has commanded "No coercion in religion (2 : 256)." It is an invitation whose objective can be fulfilled only with the free consent of the called. Since the objective is an exercise by the called of his own judgement that Allah is his Creator, Master, Lord and Judge, a forced judgement is a *contradictio in adjecto* and hence punishable with *jahannam*. Humanistic ethic regards coerced *da'wah* as a grave violation of the human person, second only to homicide, if not equal to it. That is why the Holy Qur'ān specified the means of persuasion to be used. "Argue the cause with them [the non-Muslims] with the more comely arguments" (16 : 125). If they are not convinced, they must be left alone (5 : 108; 3 : 176-177; 47 : 32). Certainly, the Muslim is to try again and never give up that God may guide his fellow-man to the truth. The example of his own life, his commitment to the values he professes, his engagement, constitue his final argument. If the non-Muslim is still not convinced, the Muslim is to rest his case with God. The Prophet himself allowed those Christians who were not convinced by his own presentation of Islam to keep their faith and return home in dignity.

From this it follows that the societal order desired by Islam is one where men are free to present and argue their religious causes with one another. It is a kind of academic seminar on a large scale where he who knows better is free to tell and to convince, and the others are free to listen and be convinced. Islam puts its trust in man's rational power to discriminate between the true and the false. "Truth is now manifest from error. Whoever believes [i.e. accepts the truth] does so for his own good. Whoever does not believe [i.e.

does not accept the truth] does so to his own peril" (39 : 41). Islamic *da'wah* is therefore an invitation to think, to debate and argue. It cannot be met with indifference except by the cynic, nor with rejection except by the fool or the malevolent. If it is met by silencing force, then that force must be met by superior force. The right to think is innate and belongs to all men. No man may preemptively deny it to any human. Islamic *da'wah* operates only under these principles. Thomas Arnold's *The Preaching of Islam* is a standing monument to *da'wah* written by a Christian missionary and colonialist.

The principle that Islamic *da'wah* is non-coercive is based upon the Qur'ān's dramatization of the justification for the creation of man. The Qur'ān represents God as addressing the angels in *Sūrat al-Baqarah*, verse 30, with the words: "Lo! I am about to place a *khalīfah* (vice-gerent) on earth. The angels replied: Will You place therein one who will do harm and will shed blood, while we sing Your praise and sanctify You? He said: Surely I know that which you know not." In another verse of the Qur'ān, *Sūrat al-Ahzāb*, 72, we read: "Lo! We offered Our trust to heaven and earth. They shrank from bearing it and were afraid of it. But man assumed it..." Both these statements are understood by Muslims as defining the purpose of man's existence, namely, that he is God's *khalīfah*, carrier of the responsibility entrusted to him for the fulfillment of the divine will. That will is already fulfilled in part, within nature as natural law, and not yet fulfilled in another part, by man as moral law. This constitutes man's distinction from all other creatures. Only he acts freely and thus enables himself to actualize the moral part of the divine will. His essence is his capacity for responsible moral action. Coercion is a violation of this freedom and responsibility, and is utterly inconsistent with man's relation to the divine will.

B. Da'wah is not a psychotropic induction

It follows from the nature of judgement that *da'wah* cannot have for objective anything but a conscientious acquiescence to its contents on the part of the called. This means that if the consciousness of the called is in any way vitiated by any of the common defaults or defects of consciousness, the *da'wah* is itself equally vitiated. Thus a *da'wah* that is fulfilled through, or whose fulfilment involves in any way, a lapse of consciousness, a lapse of forgetfulness, a lapse in *ta'aqqul* or the intellectual binding of ideas and facts so as to make a cohesive and consistent whole, or a transport of emotion and enthusiasm, a sort of "trip", is not Islamic *da'wah*. *Da'wah*, therefore, is not the work of magic, of illusion, of excitment, of any kind of psychotropia. In such work, the subject is not in control of his power of judgement, and hence, his judgement cannot be properly said to be his "personal free judgement".

The presence of God, that is as Ultimate Reality, Creator and Lord of the Universe, Judge and Master of all men, is a fact which can indeed enter common consciousness. Indeed, Islam holds that were consciousness to be tampered with, the object perceived would not be God, but something else.

Under the tremendous impact of revelation itself, the Prophet's consciousness neither lapsed nor became vague as in a mystical experience, but continued to function normally and was even enhanced in its clarity and perception. That is why Islamic law does not recognize the conversion to Islam of the minor child; for his consciousness is presumed immature until he comes of age.

The principle that da'wah has nothing to do with psychotropic induction preserves the freedom and consciousness of choice which cannot be affirmed in case of dilation of consciousness by chemical or mystifying means. It protects the da'wah from being conducted for pleasure, happiness, freedom from care, eudaemonia — indeed, for anything but the sake of Allah. Any ulterior motive would vitiate it in both the giver and the recipient. On the other hand, unconscious conversion of any person who has been tricked into entering Islam is evil; more evil, of course, is the trickster.

C. Da'wah is directed to Muslims as well as non-Muslims

It follows from the divine commandment that da'wah must be the end product of a critical process of intellection. Its content cannot be the only content known, the only content presented. For there is no judgement without consideration of alternatives, without comparison and contrast, without tests of inner consistency, of general consistency with all other knowledge, without tests of correspondence with reality. It is this aspect of da'wah that earns for the called who responds affirmatively to its content the grace of Hikmah or wisdom. Allah (s.w.t.) described His prophets and saints as "Men of Hikmah" precisely because their Islam was a learned thing, not a narrow-minded addiction to a single track of thought, certainly not a "pre-judgement". That is why da'wah in Islam has never been thought of as exclusively addressed to the non-Muslims. It is as much intended for the benefit of Muslims as of non-Muslims.

Besides stemming from the fact of all men's equal creatureliness in front of God, this universalism of da'wah rests on the identity of imperative arising out of conversion to Islam. All men stand under the obligation to actualize the divine pattern in space and time. This task is never complete for any individual. The Muslim is supposedly the person who, having accepted the burden, has set himself on the road of actualization. The non-Muslim still has to accept the charge. Hence, da'wah is necessarily addressed to both, to the Muslim to press forward toward actualization and to the non-Muslim to join the ranks of those who make the pursuit of God's pattern supreme.

The directing of da'wah to Muslim as much as non-Muslims is indicative of the fact that, unlike Christianity, Islamicity is never a fait accompli. Islamicity is a process. It grows, and it is sometimes reduced. There is no time at which the Muslim may carry his title to paradise, as it were, in his pocket. Instead of "salvation", the Muslim is to achieve felicity through unceasing effort.

D. Da'wah is rational intellection

Since *da'wah* is a critical process of intellection, it is of its nature never to be dogmatic, never to stand by its contents as if by its own authority, or that of its mouthpiece, or that of its tradition. For it to be critical means that it should keep itself always open to new evidence, to new alternatives; that it continually cast and recast itself in new forms, in cognizance of the new discoveries of human science, of the new needs of human situation. In making the *da'wah*, the *dā'iyah* labours not as the ambassador of an authoritarian system, but as the co-thinker who is co-operating with the *mad'ū* (the called) in the understanding and appreciation of Allah's double revelation, in creation and through His Prophets. So much for the standpoint of the *dā'iyah*.

From the standpoint of the *mad'ū*, his process of intellection should never stop. His *īmān* should be dynamic and always growing in intensity, clarity of vision and comprehensiveness. Moreover, conversion to Islam is not a sacrament which, once it takes place, becomes an eternal *fait accompli*. Islam knows of no "justification by faith", certainly of no "justification" in the sense of *justi facti*. If lethargic and stagnant, *īmān* degenerates into narrow-mindedness and gradually impoverishes its subject. On the other hand, its dynamism — its openness to new knowledge, new evidence and new life-situations, new data, problems, as well as creative solutions which may or may not be derived from the tradition — makes it a source of enrichment for the subject. Fortunate is he whose *īmān* increases in *"yaqīn-ness"* (certitude) with every new day.

As rational intellection, *da'wah* shows that in Islam, faith has to do with knowledge and conviction, whereas in Christianity it is, as Pascal found out, a blind wager. The Arabic word *īmān* does not mean "faith" as Christians use the term. Rather, it means "conviction". It does not involve the functioning of a sacrament. There is no *ex opere operata* principle in Islam.

E. Da'wah is rationally necessary

Islamic *da'wah* is therefore the presentation of rational, i.e. critical, truth. It is not the proclamation of an event, or even of a truth (idea), but the presentation, for critical assessment as to truth value, of a proposition, a factum, which has theoretical (metaphysical) and practical (ethical) relevance for man. As to the recalcitrant will, Islam recognized it for what it is, namely, recalcitrant and delinquent, and left the subject of that will to himself until God guides him to the truth. It respected his will and his judgement and, indeed, it extended to him its protections and *Pax Islamica*. But it asked him to respond equally with peace and not to interfere with his neighbor's right to listen and be convinced. Moreover, the Muslim of history has always presented his case in the open, never entered or practiced his Islam in secret. His *da'wah* preceded his entry onto any international or interreligious scene. In consequence, he interpreted the killing of the *dā'iyah*, the silencing of his *da'wah*, as a hostile act, a rejection of the peaceful call to reason and argument, and not merely the opposition of a recalcitrant will. That is also why, once his call is answered not with conversion but merely with "yea, I will think", the Muslim of history has spared absolutely nothing in so presenting his argument as to make it convincing; above all, by embodying it forth in its universalism, justice and brotherhood.

That da'wah is rationally necessary is implied by the fact that in presenting its case, Islam presents it as natural or rational truth. "Rational" here means "critical". Men differ in their use of reason but there would be no point to our dialogue unless we assume the truth to be knowable, that is, unless we believe it possible to arrive at principles which overarch our differences. Therefore, the standpoint of Islam is not an "act of faith", but one of "conviction". It is one of knowledge, of trust in the human power to know.

F. Da'wah is anamnesis

In commanding the Muslim to call men to the path of Allah, He *(s.w.t.)* did not ask him to call men to anything new, to something which is foreign or unknown to them. Islam is *dīn al-fitrah (religio naturalis)* which is already present in its fullness in man by nature. It is innate, as it were, a natural constituent of humanity. The man who is not *homo religiosus*, and hence *homo Islamicus*, is not a man. This is Allah's branding of His creation, namely, that He has endowed all men, as His creatures, with a *sensus numinus*, a *fitrah*, with which to recognize Him as Allah (God), Transcendent Creator, Ultimate Master, and One. It is history which confirms this natural faculty with its primeval perceptions and intellections, cultivates and enriches it or warps it and diverts it from its natural goal.

Da'wah is the call of man to return to himself, to what is innate in him, to "objective" or "phenemenological" (i.e. with suspension of the indoctrinations and inculcations of history) reexamination of facts which are already given, and so in him. It is the nearest thing to Platonic *anamnesis* without the absurdity of reincarnation or transmigration of souls. As such, the claims of *da'wah* are necessarily moderate, nay humble! For the *dā'iyah* is to do no more than the "midwife", to stir the intellect of the *mad'ū* to rediscover what he already knows, the innate knowledge which God has implanted in him at birth.

As *anamnesis*, *da'wah* is based upon the Islamic assertion that primeval religion or monotheism is found in every man *(dīn al-fitrah)*, and that all he needs is to be reminded of it. The function of the prophets is to remind people of what is already in them. Christianity has approached this position in the literature of the Apostolic Fathers and particularly in the Enlightenment. But it receded from this position in the nineteenth century because western man was too deeply commited to his ethno-centrism to accept the universalism implied in that position. Let us remember that Immanuel Kant, the prince of the Enlightenment, held that "to be black is an argument", and categorized the world's races in order of ascendency with the Europeans on top. This was a failure of nerve on the part of Christendom.

37

G. Da'wah is ecumenical par excellence

Islam's discovery of *dīn al-fitrah* and its vision of it as base of all historical religion is a breakthrough of tremendous importance in interreligious relations. For the first time it has become possible to hold adherents of all other religions as equal members of a universal religious brotherhood. All religious traditions are *de jure*, for they have all issued from and are based upon a common source, the religion of God which He has implanted equally in all men, upon *dīn al-fitrah*. The problem is to find out how far the religious traditions agree with *dīn al-fitrah*, the original and first religion; the problem is to trace the historical development of religions and determine precisely how and when and where each has followed and fulfilled, or transcended and deviated from, *dīn al-fitrah*. Holy writ as well as all other religious texts must be examined in order to discover what change has befallen them, or been reflected in them, in history. Islam's breakthrough is thus the first call to scholarship in religion, to critical analysis of religious texts, of the claim of such texts to revelation status. It is the first call to the discipline of "history of religions" because it was the first to assume that all religions had a history, that each religion has undergone a development.

Islam does not claim for itself, therefore, the status of a novelty, but of a fact and dispensation at least as old as creation. The religious life of man, with all its variety across the ages is rehabilitated under this view not as a series of vagaries, but as attempts at true religion. Monotheism is said to be as old as creation.

Islamic *da'wah* begins by reaffirming this ultimate base as genuine and true. It seeks to complete the critical task of sifting in the accumulated traditions the wheat from the chaff. We are not impressed by the claim of latter-day ecumenists, advocates of interreligious dialogue, toleration and co-existence, who assert the ultimacy of any religious system because it is religious. For such a claim is the absolutization of every religion's propositions, which is nothing short of cultural relativism. Indeed, such ecumenism is non-representative of the religions which claim that what they propose is *the* truth, and not merely *a* claim to the truth among many claims. And it is rationally inconsequential because it counsels the juxtaposition in consciousness of contrary claims to the truth without the demand for a solution of their contradiction. By avoiding all these pitfalls and shortcomings, Islamic *da'wah* is ecumenical, if ecumenicity is to have any meaning besides kitchen cooperation among the churches.

Da'wah is ecumenical *par excellence* because it regards any kind of intercourse between the Muslim and the non-Muslim as a domestic relationship between kin. The Muslim comes to the non-Muslim and says "we are one ; we are one family under Allah, and Allah has given you the truth not only inside yourself but inside your religious tradition which is *de jure* because its source is in God.". The task of dialogue, or mission, is thus transformed into one of sifting the history of the religion in question. *Da'wah* thus becomes an

38

ecumenical cooperative critique of the other religion rather than its invasion by a new truth.

II. Da'wah Content

Islam's view of other faiths flows from the essence of its religious experience. This essence is critically knowable. It is not the subject of "paradox", nor of "continuing revelation", nor the object of construction or reconstruction by Muslims. It is crystallized in the Holy Qur'ān for all men to read. It is clearly comprehensible to the man of today as it was to that of Arabia of the Prophet's day (570-632 A.C.) because the categories of grammar, lexicography, syntax and redaction of the Qur'ānic text, and those of Arabic consciousness embedded in the Arabic language, have not changed through the centuries. This phenomenon is indeed unique; for Arabic is the only language which remained the same for nearly two millennia, the last fourteen centuries of which being certainly due to the Holy Qur'ān.[1] For Muslims, this essence has been on every lip and in every mind, every hour of every day.

The essence of Islam is *tawhīd* or the witnessing that there is no god but God. Brief as it is, this witness packs into itself four principles which constitute the whole essence and ultimate foundation of the religion.

First, that there is no god but God means that reality is dual, consisting of a natural realm, the realm of creation, and a transcendent realm, the Creator. This principle distinguishes Islam from trinitarian Christianity where the dualism of creator and creature is maintained but where it is combined with a divine immanentism in human nature in justification of the incarnation. *Tawhīd* requires that neither nature be apotheosized nor transcendent God be objectified, the two realities ever-remaining ontologically disparate.

Second, *tawhīd* means that God is related to what is not God as its God, that is, as its creator or ultimate cause, its master or ultimate end. Creator and creature, therefore, *tawhīd* asserts, are relevant to each other regardless of their ontological disparateness which is not affected by the relation. The transcendent Creator, being cause and final end of the natural creature, is the ultimate Master Whose will is the religious and moral imperative. The divine will is commandment and law, the "ought" of all that is, knowable by the direct means of revelation, or the indirect means of rational and/or empirical analysis of what is. Without a knowable content, the divine will would not be normative or imperative, and hence would not be the final end of the natural; for if the transcendent Creator is not the final end of His

---

[1] Controversies have arisen, as they certainly may, in the interpretation of the Qur'ānic text. What is being affirmed here is the fact that the Qur'ānic text is not bedevilled by a hermeneutical problem. Differences of interpretation are apodictically soluble in terms of the very same categories of understanding in force at the time of revelation of the text (611-632 A. C.), all of which have continued the same because of the freezing of the language and the daily intercourse of countless millions of people with it and with the text of the Holy Qur'ān.

own creature, creation must be not the purposive event consonant with divine nature but a meaningless happening to Him, a threat to His own ultimacy and transcendence.

Thirdly, *tawhīd* means that man is capable of action, that creation is malleable or capable of receiving man's action, and that human action on malleable nature, resulting in a transformed creation, is the purpose of religion. Contrary to the claims of other religions, nature is neither fallen or evil, nor a sort of *Untergang* of the absolute, nor is the absolute an apotheosis of it. Both are real, and both are good — the Creator being the *summum bonum* and the creature being intrinsically good and potentially better as it is transformed by human action into the pattern the Creator has willed for it. We have already seen that knowledge of the divine will is possible for man; and through revelation and science such knowledge is actual. The prerequisites of the transformation of creation into the likeness of the divine pattern are hence all, but for human resolve and execution, fulfilled and complete.

Fourthly, *tawhīd* means that man, alone among all the creatures, is capable of action as well as free to act or not to act. This freedom vests him with a distinguishing quality, namely responsibility. It casts upon his action its moral character; for the moral is precisely that which is done in freedom, i.e., done by an agent who is capable of doing, as well as of not doing, it. This kind of action, moral action, is the greater portion of the divine will. Being alone capable of it, man is a higher creature, endowed with the cosmic significance of that through whose agency alone is the higher part of the divine will to be actualized in space and time. Man's life on earth, therefore, is especially meaningful and cosmically significant. As Allah has put it in the Holy Qur'ān, man is God's *khalīfah*, or vice-gerent on earth.[2] It is of the nature of moral action that its fulfillment be not equivalent to its non-fulfillment, that man's exercise of his freedom in actualizing the divine imperative be not without difference. Hence, another principle is necessary, whereby successful moral action would meet with happiness and its opposite with unhappiness. Otherwise it would be all one for man whether he acts, or does not act, morally. Indeed, this consideration makes judgement necessary, in which the total effect of one's lifetime activity is assessed and its contribution to the total value of the cosmos is acknowledged, imbalances in the individual's life are redressed and his achievement is distinguished from the non-achievement of others. This is what "The Day of Judgement" and "Paradise and Hell" are meant to express in religious language.

Fifthly, *tawhīd* means the commitment of man to enter into the nexus of nature and history, there to actualize the divine will. It understands that will as pro-world and pro-life and hence, it mobilizes all human energies in the service of culture and civilization. Indeed, it is of its essence to be a civilizing force. In consequence, Islamic *da'wah* is not based upon a condemnation of the world.

---

2 Qur'ān 2 : 30; 6 : 165; 10 : 14, 73; 35 : 39; 7 : 68, 73; 27 : 62.

It does not justify itself as a call to man to relieve himself from the predicament of an existence which it regards as suffering and misery. Its urgency is not an assumed "need for salvation" or for compassion and deliverance from anything. In this, as in the preceding aspects, Islamic *da'wah* differs from that of Christianity. Assuming all men necessarily to be "fallen", to stand in the predicament of "original sin", of "alienation from God", of self-contradiction, self-centeredness, or of "falling short of the perfection of God", Christian mission seeks to ransom and save. Islam holds man to be not in need of any salvation. Instead of assuming him to be religiously and ethically fallen, Islamic *da'wah* acclaims him as the *khalīfah* of Allah, perfect in form, and endowed with all that is necessary to fulfill the divine will indeed, even loaded with the grace of revelation! "Salvation" is hence not in the vocabulary of Islam. *Falāh*, or the positive achievement in space and time of the divine will, is the Islamic counterpart of Christian "deliverance" and "redemption".

The Islamic *da'wah* does not, therefore, call man to a phantasmagoric second or other kingdom which is an alternative to this one, but to assume his natural birthright, his place as the maker of history, as the remolder and refashioner of creation. Equally, his joys and pleasures are all his to enjoy, his life to live and his will to exercise, since the content of the divine will is not "not-of-this-world", but "of it". World-denial and life-abnegation, asceticism and monasticism, isolationism and individualism, subjectivism and relativism are not virtues in Islam but *dalāl* (misguidance). Islam stands squarely within the Mesopotamian religious tradition where religion is civilization and civilization is religion.

Finally, *tawhīd* restores to man a dignity which some religions have denied by their representation of him as "fallen", as existentially miserable. By calling him to exercise his God-given prerogatives, Islamic *da'wah* rehabilitates him and reestablishes his sanity, innocence and dignity. His moral vocation is the road to his *falāh*. Certainly the Muslim is called to a new theocentrism; but it is one in which man's cosmic dignity is applauded by Allah and His Angels. Christianity calls man to respond with faith to the salvific act of God and seeks to rehabilitate man by convincing him that it is he for whom God has shed His own blood. Man, it asserts, is certainly great because he is God's partner whom God would not allow to destroy himself. This is indeed greatness, but it is the greatness of a helpless puppet. Islam understands itself as man's assumption of his cosmic role as the one for whose sake creation was created. He is its innocent, perfect and moral master; and every part of it is *his* to have and to enjoy. He is called to obey, i.e. to fulfil the will of Allah. But this fulfilment is in and of space and time precisely because Allah is the source of space and time and the moral law.

Man, as Islam defines him, is not an object of salvation, but its subject. Through his agency alone the moral part, which is the higher part of the will of God, enters, and is fulfilled in, creation. In a sense, therefore, man is God's partner, but a partner worthy of God because he is trustworthy as His *khalīfa*, not because he is pitifully helpless and needs to be "saved".

. . . .

Khurshid Ahmad opened the discussion of Dr. al-Faruqi's paper with the following prepared response. Some parts of a background paper he circulated at the consultation have also been incorporated in this final version. (Editors)

Ahmad: First of all I would like to compliment Professor Ismaᶜil al-Faruqi on his short but brilliant exposition of Islamic *daᶜwah*. This paper brings to sharp focus the real nature of the Islamic *daᶜwah* and some of its salient features. Another significant aspect of this exposition is that it also emphasizes, albeit indirectly, some important elements of the *modus vivendi* of the Islamic *daᶜwah*. I fully agree with the substance of Professor al-Faruqi's argument as well as with his formulation of the issues involved.

After this introductory observation, I would like to say a few words about three aspects of Islamic *daᶜwah*, that is, its *what*, *why* and *how*.

The central issue, according to Islam, is not man's need to know the person of God and to extricate himself from his vicarious predicament by seeking the grace of a saviour, but his need for *hidāyah* (divine guidance) to enable him to know the will of God and to try to live in obedience to it. Islam means complete submission to the Divine Will and it is this harmonization of man's will with the Divine Will that leads to real peace — peace within man's soul, between man and man, between man and the creation and finally between man and God.

The human situation, according to the Islamic view, is exemplified in the Qur'ānic narration about the creation of man. He was created to play a positive and dynamic role — that of God's *khalīfah*, His deputy, representative and vice-gerent on earth. He was endowed with free will, with the capacity to make moral decisions, and was given the knowledge of things, so as to make such decisions properly. He was given the opportunity to make moral decisions for himself and to show whether he can behave responsibly, fulfilling the trust put in him. The experience he had with this freedom before he came to the earth brings to light his potentialities as well as his weaknesses — his exposure to evil and the dangers of his succumbing to it, as also his innate goodness to realize his mistakes and to strive to rectify them. It is because of this human situation that man needs divine guidance — as a reminder, a protector and a guide to make the right moral decision and remain steadfast in this respect. The critical question is man's relationship with God and in the light of that his relationship with himself, with other human beings, with the entire creation and with history.

The strategy of the *hidāyah* is to start with giving to man the *īmān*, that is, faith and conviction in the unity of God — in *tawhīd* with all its ramifications. God is One. He is the Creator, the Lord, the Mercy-Giving, the Sustainer,

42

the Nourisher, the Perfector, the Truth, the Guide, the Law-Giver, the Sovereign, the Judge, the One to whom is man's return. God and man represent two categories and man's success and salvation lies in accepting God as his God, as *Ma'būd* (the object of worship, reverence, loyalty and obedience).

God's will is not something mysterious, unknown or vague. It is revealed in the *hidāyah* which provides the code for human conduct, the Law, the *sharī'ah*. Islam is a complete way of life — *al-dīn*. Acceptance of God and His *hidāyah* results in the emergence of a community of faith. Social institutions are reared on the foundations of *īmān*. Muslim community is an ideological entity and represents a social movement to actualize in space and time the demands of the *hidāyah*.

Islam is not merely a metaphysical doctrine or a theology; in it emphasis is on *īmān* as the starting point, that is a conviction and a commitment to accept God as the Lord and to submit to His Will completely. This produces a particular outlook on life. Islam also provides a complete way of life; a system with explicit criteria for right and wrong and a set of clear injunctions as to how to regulate major institutions of human society. Finally, Islam inculcates the spirit of living in God's presence as symbolized in the Islamic value of *ihsān*.

In this scheme, the prophets of God were not merely passive recipients and simple communicators of divine guidance but were also assigned the responsibility of presenting before man a living model of that guidance, a model that could be followed and emulated by divine sanction. All prophets of God fulfilled this function and Prophet Muhammad (peace be upon him) represents the last expression of this model. The Qur'ān contains the Word of God as it was revealed to the Prophet, and his *sunnah* provides the living model which we as Muslims try to follow and to approximate to.

This being the framework, we are now in a position to answer briefly the three questions we posed at the outset. The *what* of the Islamic *da'wah* means invitation to Islam as a faith and as a way of life, as *al-dīn*. This is an invitation to all human beings and the invitation becomes more pressing for those who respond to this call, for they have to engage themselves in an unceasing struggle to transform their own lives, individual and social, in accordance with this code of guidance. It is an invitation not only to a new *īmān*, a new outlook in life, but also to a new order, the Islamic way of life. It is an invitation, not merely to the acceptance of a certain historical event, but to engage in a dynamic and unceasing process of understanding, training and social action, towards the transformation of human life through *tarbiyah* and *tazkiyah*, to suggest the relevant Islamic values.

The *why* of the *da'wah* can be understood by reflecting upon the framework we have discussed. Man is not self-sufficient and needs divine guidance. As Muhammad (peace be upon him) is the last Prophet, how does the mechanism for guidance operate after him? The Islamic position is that this is ensured first by the preservation of the divine guidance in its pure and pristine form in the Qur'ān and secondly by making the Muslim *ummah* — every Muslim and all Muslims — the witness of Truth before mankind in the same way as the Prophet was a witness of the Truth unto them.[1] This has also been enjoined upon the Muslims in a number of places in the Qur'ān as also by the Prophet.[2]

Now a word about the *how*. *Da'wah* is presented primarily through conveying the message, preaching you may call it, and by practising it and as such presenting before the world its living example. Islam has ruled out techniques of coercion as instruments of *da'wah*. The methods it has enjoined and actualized in history are methods of communication, discussion and persuasion on the one hand, and the gravitational pull of godliness as exemplified in the lives of the people and realized in the social order. There is no professional class of priests or preachers in Islam. Every Muslim is responsible for the *da'wah* whatever be his vocation in life.

Fitzgerald: I would like to ask for clarification of Dr al-Faruqi's statement that Islamic *da'wah* is ecumenical *par excellence*, by virtue of its comprehensive recognition of all the religions as *de jure*. In fact, what is meant by *all* religions? Having recourse to Apollo and other gods and goddesses is a kind of religion, but would Islam recognize this as well as all other religions as *de jure*?

al-Faruqi: Islam recognizes all religions as *de jure*, and then it invites the adherents of these religions to begin the task of criticism. No religion is ruled out by the Muslim *a priori*. In other words, if I meet someone who has never heard of Islam and who worships, for example, an "X" or "Y", whatever that may be, I as a Muslim am not free to call him a pagan, or to regard him as condemned by God; rather, I must talk with him in order to discover what his religion is, in the belief that God must in His mercy have sent a prophet to him, for the Qur'ān says: "And there is no people unto whom God has not sent a prophet" (Q. 35 : 24).

Believing then that God in His mercy must have told him something, I meet with him with a view to being instructed about his faith, and then I invite him to research his own tradition in order to discover the essential message that God has given him. And if, in relation to that central revealed core, the rest of the beliefs and practices of that religion as developed through history turn out to be a pack of lies, that would be an empirical discovery for me. But for the Muslim this must never be an *a priori* decision which condemns a man because he doesn't believe "in my God my way"!

However, if I discover that another man's religion has been corrupted and falsified beyond recognition, then I have a duty to tell him about the Qur'ān,

---

[1] Qur'ān 2 : 143; also 22 : 78.
[2] Qur'ān 3 : 104; also 3 : 110.

44

God's final revelation, to present it to him as rational truth, and invite his consideration. If he says, "I don't want to listen", then either he is malevolent or a fool.

Cragg: What you are saying, then, is that God has sent prophets everywhere, but *ex hypothesi* these prophets must be consistent with Islam.

al-Faruqi: Yes, Islam as *religio naturalis, dīn al-fitrah*.

Cragg: But that which in Buddhism is antithetical to Islam and to rationalism is not simply chaff mixed with wheat, if I may put it that way; it is the very wheat of Buddhism. By your analysis here it must then have been a false prophecy which brought the Buddhist to that belief.

al-Faruqi: I won't say a false prophecy. I would say that a true revelation through an authentic prophet has been thoroughly falsified.

Fitzeragld: But by what historical criteria is the "true" prophet to be identified? And where is the "true" prophecy of which you speak within Buddhism?

al-Faruqi: I don't know, but it can be researched; the fact that I assume it to be there at the origin is at least a good step in the direction of ecumenical tolerance.

Ahmad: It is very possible that rudiments of the true prophecy are to be found even in some pagan religions.

Cragg: It seems rather an escape hatch of a theory, because if a prophet is really a prophet then his message becomes known, it is *balāgh*, communication; and if it has not survived historically it must be mythical.

al-Faruqi: No. At one time it was known. But then later on it became falsified as the Hebrew message became falsified, and the Christian message was falsified.

Cragg: But from an historical point of view that would be entirely conjectural.

The discussion then turned to Dr al-Faruqi's point that Islamic da'wah is "rational intellection". (Editors)

Cragg: Going back to your exegesis of the verse in *Surat al-Ahzāb*, we take the point that there is a kind of natural Islam of nature — that is, *islām* with a small "i", as it were — and there is a volitional Islam, on the part of man. But in the conclusion of that verse, after man has accepted the trust, the Qur'ān says: "Indeed he is a wrong doer and rebellious" — which is what the Psalms describe when they speak of the "froward", i.e. both ill-advised and obstinate. It is this area that I am so deeply concerned about in your paper because, if I may put it this way, there is a certain naïveté about principles of reason, and about your alternative of the world being either full of fools or of people who are prepared to be persuaded. Is there not a third possibility that there is a kind of quality of ... perverseness? — for which law, exhortation, argument, do not suffice. Indeed they may provoke the very disobedience they condemn. Could it not be that it is this perversity of man which is implied in that particular verse in the Qur'ān? There seems to be a real emphasis upon man as being in trust and at the same time distorting the trust he was given; the trust, if you like, is simply the context of the distortion. Your paper, in its very real concern which we all share for a right and true humanism, neglects this dimension which, perhaps in some emphases exaggeratedly, nevertheless essentially has been at the core of the Christian tradition about man, and the sense of the divine responsibility which Christians understand in terms of that saving intervention which you say is psychotropic folly . . . or whatever.

al-Faruqi: Since we understand the purport of this verse as being to stress the moral aspect of the will of God, it stands to reason that the violation of it is mentioned in the verse rather than its realization. But the realization is mentioned in many other verses in the Qur'ān. The concern here is not really with man's violation as something necessary, but with man's violation as something real. Nobody can deny that men sin and do evil. They are not angels. In the other verse of the Qur'ān which I quoted, the angels actually argue with God that men will sin. But God says that He has a motive in creating man which the angels do not know. The difference between Islam and Christianity is still very great here. Islam recognizes the universality of sin, and God deals with it by sending down the Qur'ān. He commands the Muslims to continue to deal with it by *da'wah*. But the concept of the necessity of sin, the fallenness of man, has nothing to do with Islam. To read in this verse any such meaning would be contrary to the meaning intended and the unanimous wisdom of fourteen centuries of Islamic thought.

Fitzgerald: Does the term "rational intellection" refer only to the *da'wah* itself or does it include also the response to *da'wah*? And of what nature is this response? Is it in any way comparable to "conversion"? In certain Christian religious philosophies, for example Thomism or Neo-Thomism, there is something similar to the idea of *dīn al-fitrah*. Man is said to be capable of the infinite; he does not have a limited horizon, but is always striving to surpass the horizon. But he is faced by a fundamental choice — he has to choose the good which is outside himself, and this is an option which has to be confirmed throughout the whole of life. If a man stops, and turns in on himself, then he is refusing his own nature. Now this sense of conversion has been described by C. S. Lewis in his autobiography as "joy", which includes an element of ecstasy. It is not therefore entirely rational, but this does not mean to say that it is irrational, rather that it is non-rational.

Bishop Rudvin took the discussion back to Dr al-Faruqi's comments about the Christian idea of sin: (Editors)

Rudvin: Comment has recently been made on the dogma of original sin. Now I was brought up in the Christian denomination — Lutheran — which has probably been the most emphatic in its insistence upon the dogma of original sin, and I would say that Dr al-Faruqi's understanding of it is not really correct. He infers that it is a necessary trait of creation, but this is exactly what it is not. The whole conception of original sin, or the fall, in Christianity is an insistence that man's empirical situation today, which is hopeless and sinful, is not a part of creation. The dogma about original sin means that we see man as he is empirically, and we emphatically deny that he was created that way.

al-Faruqi: But you define the state of innocence as Adam before the fall — well, that is not history, and what troubles me is that Christianity declares all men to be sinful in essence throughout the entire history of creation. The fall in Christian thought means that all men are by nature sinful, not just that all men sin in the same way as we might say that all men have noses! The fall means guilt, crime, and Christianity seems to condemn all men as being necessarily criminals, necessarily guilty.

Rudvin: But here you are presenting your own conclusions as the substance of Christian doctrine. I would summarize the whole doctrine of original sin like this: we recognize that empirical and practical man is in an awful mess, and all men are in the same mess, and have been throughout history, but we deny — or we insist, we cry out — that this is not what man was created to be. Man is not a sinner of necessity, but by his own will.

Sanneh: I would like to approach this issue from another direction — from the angle of revelation. The problem of revelation is not just the question of divine initiative — God willing and wanting to reveal himself to man in the form of a code of laws — but it is also intertwined with the problem of human volition and how man has resisted, indeed rebelled against, and sometimes persecuted the spokesmen of God, the prophets. Muhammad came as a reminder, certainly, which underscores the idea of Islam as *din al-fitrah*; but he came also as a *warner* — a warner because man is recalcitrant, a disputatious being who will argue with the divine initiative and struggle against it. The Qur'ān itself accepts the problem that to secure man's obedience is itself a highly ambiguous and problematic issue, because the intent to seek man's obedience carries with it the risk of man's refusing to give his obedience.

In answer to Dr Sanneh, Dr al-Faruqi opened up an area of fascinating discussion: (Editors)

al-Faruqi: You spoke of God "willing and wanting to reveal Himself to man". God does *not* reveal Himself. He does not reveal Himself to anyone in any way. God reveals only His will. Remember one of the prophets asked God to reveal Himself and God told him, "No, it is not possible for Me to reveal Myself to anyone."

Cragg: Do you make this distinction absolute? Is not the will expressive of the nature?

al-Faruqi: Only the nature *in percipe*. In other words, the will of God is God *in percipe* — the nature of God in so far as I can know anything about Him.

47

This is God's will and that is all we have — and we have it in perfection in the Qur'ān. But Islam does not equate the Qur'ān with the nature or essence of God. It is the Word of God, the Commandment of God, the Will of God. But God does not reveal Himself to anyone. Christians talk about the revelation of God Himself — by God of God — but that is the great difference between Christianity and Islam. God is transcendent, and once you talk about self-revelation you have hierophancy and immanence, and then the transcendence of God is compromised. You may not have complete transcendence and self-revelation at the same time.

Cragg: But no more can you have complete transcendence and creation.

al-Faruqi: Yes, you can. Because creation is, in the Qur'ān's words, *kun fa yaqun*, "be and it is". Creation is a commandment of God (Q. 3 : 47 *et al.*).

Cragg: Yes, but the creation of man is an involvement of the divine will with the human answer, as Dr Sanneh has been arguing. And therefore it is possible to say that to some extent the transcendent is now in the custody of man.

al-Faruqi: But God created creation by His command. I as a creature have no right to inflate myself and the rest of creation to such a degree as to say that without His creation God would flounder.

Cragg: But if I may say so modestly, you proceed into an extravagance. The point we are trying to get at is whether in Islam there is a divine responsibility — as I believe there is — and I believe this binds Christians and Muslims very closely together — a divine responsibility relating to this creation and to man in particular. This is, I believe, the proper corollary of a belief in creation, and of a belief in revelation and the succession of prophets. God cares about being obeyed and seeks the obedience through the sequence of prophets. Now we on the Christian side are going to go further and say: Yes, God seeks this obedience in redemptive terms. But I'll leave that aside for the moment. The principle must surely be established that the will of God is involved in the creation, and therefore involved in man the creature, offering him the trust (*amānah*) and giving him the vice-gerency (*khilāfah*). God, so to speak, has gone out on a limb. The omnipotence of God is, we could say, in a certain sense compromised, to the extent that an element of what this omnipotence is seeking is now squarely entrusted to man.

al-Faruqi: Not really. I as a human being can create a computer or an automaton to do certain things and not to do other things, but the existence of the automaton is certainly no compromise of my own inventive power or my superior mind.

Cragg: But your analogy breaks down. Man is not a computer. As you yourself said in an earlier session, he is a volitional being and what is required of him is a volitional Islam. This cannot be automatic, for it must always turn upon the will of man.

Ahmad: I do not see the logic of saying that because God has created man as a volitional being His Omnipotence and Sovereignty are in any way compromised. God can be caring. God is caring. But that doesn't mean that He abandons part of His Sovereignty or Transcendence. On the one hand, as we find in the Qur'ān, God is caring and loving — *Rahmān, Rahīm, Wadūd* — and He desires man's obedience and worship; but on the other hand the Qur'ān also makes it clear that God is in no way dependent or in need of man's worship. If men refuse to worship God and to obey Him, God is not affected. It is not God Who seeks completion in our worship, but rather we who seek completion through worshipping Him.

Cragg: Now we have really come to something which is crucial. In my view if you want an unmitigated transcendence, then you have got to go to Buddhism where the absolute is totally dissociated from the immanent and historical. But unmitigated transcendence for me is a contradiction in terms. I have introduced the term "compromise", which is an unfortunate term because it suggests bargaining with truth. But if we are going to use this word, then it would seem to me that an indifferent transcendence would be the compromise. It is not that God cares and comes that compromises him. The abeyance of this would compromise him because it would be a kind of abdication.

If I may say so, it seems to me that what we have to try to do is to think more deeply about what we mean by omnipotence. Omnipotence is not the ability to do all things, but rather the ability to be undefeated. It means that God will subdue all things unto himself. It means a final competence. But having said this, I as a Christian am of the conviction that there are certain things about which we can say: "God ought". I find it a terribly desolating and finally contradictory concept to believe in unobligated deity. That is deism. Theism, to which we here are all committed, must mean divine involvement for this, as I have said, is implicit in creation itself. You cannot create and be as if you hadn't. You cannot have law and be indifferent to what happens to it. You cannot educate and be indifferent to what is happening in education. The whole succession of prophets seems to argue a divine solicitude; *jāhiliyyah* matters. If you have a false God it matters. Now this is not a fiction; it is not a play on words. God is involved in wrong that *jāhiliyyah* does to him. I would say that this is where, if we are open together, Islam has to be open at a deep level to what Christians are saying, just as we Christians want to be open to what you are saying. Can we think of the *Allāhu akbar* as a genuine accountability and responsibility to the human situation? Is not that within the meaning of transcendence?

al-Faruqi: No. Allah is not responsible for our misdeeds.

Cragg: ... If he isn't, quite simply I would prefer to be an atheist. An indifferent or a silent heaven ...

al-Faruqi: I would deny accountability or responsibility on the part of God for my misdeeds. I do not mean to say that God is indifferent, that God is a cynic. Of course He cares. But God has given me freedom and moral responsibility. He has given me all the equipment needed for knowing His will, and even if I am lethargic of mind He has given me the quick rule of thumb by which to know His will — the *shari'ah*, the law, which I can read easily in books. Now if it is my will, despite all this, to disobey Him, then I am responsible and I have to bear the burden — not God. How can the Judge, how can the Source of the law, how can the King be responsible for the misdeeds of the subject? But of course if His citizenry turns out to be gangsters, He will use His authority as Judge and King. Men do fail in their responsibilities — this is an uncontrovertible, empirical fact — and Islam recognizes it fully. The Qur'ān tells us that God is Merciful, and that it is out of His mercy and grace that He has given us revelation through the prophets in order to correct us.

Cragg: Well, I think that we are agreed that transcendence is not non-involvement. What is at issue is the degree of this involvement ...

al-Faruqi: The kind of involvement... not the degree. The nature of involvement.

Cragg: But the Qur'ān says *kataba 'alā nafsihi al-rahmah* — "He has written the mercy upon his soul" (Q. 6 : 12). Now that is a verse which takes the will of God into the nature of God. Let's take the metaphor of a shepherd, for example. What is the degree of his responsibility? We think of shepherd-hood as requiring the utmost of exposure, search, compassion, concern, and would not think a shepherd responsible if he were to say: "Here I have got a fold, and I will sit in it folding my hands." However, whatever a shepherd does under the constraint of his nature is not limitation: it is fulfilment. It would be the repudiation of this which would constitute limitation.

Here we are talking about the degree of the divine relationship to the human predicament. On the one hand you say there is a divine involvement because God cares about man, but his relationship is didactic, hortatory, educational — revelatory in terms of propositions. But is there the possibility of a relationship more tragic, more compassionate? We are not wanting to say that God is less great but differently greater. Now let God be God. It is possible that you can be found forbidding things to God in the interest of what you think is his dignity, and we ought to beware of this.

al-Faruqi: I am forbidding man, not forbidding God.

Cragg: But you are forbidding God, implicitly at least, for you say there are things that it is not appropriate for God to do. You are forbidding God the sovereign freedom of manifesting his transcendence in whatever way he choose — which may be to condescend to man's condition in terms of incarnation. What I am saying is, let God himself be the arbiter of what is appropriate to transcendence. This is all I am pleading for.

al-Faruqi: What does this mean, "Let God be the arbiter of his transcendence"? After all there is this revealed text in the Qur'ān which says: *laisa kamithlihi* *shay* — "there is nothing like unto Him" (Q. 42 : 11). It is we who must beware of what is appropriate when talking about God and about transcendence.

Rudvin: If care means that you are really involved, then what you care for affects you ... it may even hurt you and cause you to suffer.

Ahmad: Again you are treating God at a human level.

al-Faruqi: In no way can God be hurt. If you want to use the word "hurt" poetically, maybe I will wink my eye and let it go ... with plenty of poetry! But if you start saying that something hurts God, therefore He has to take action, then I say that you are putting a condition upon the divinity of God.

Cragg: But if you say anything about God, if you use any human description of him, then you are by implication making God share in humanness. So you are involved in the paradox if you are to use the divine names at all. This is not at stake between us. Once again, the question is the degree to which one can interpret the status of the divine self-spending, which is the heart of the Christian faith — "Being in the form of God he took upon himself the form of a servant". You mentioned kingship a moment ago. We have a marvellous example of kingship in Shakespeare in *Henry V*, when the king lays the crown aside and shows a simple concern to get alongside the common soldier in a dire situation. Is this less kingly than sitting in the palace on a throne? I think most of us would agree that it is not.

Al-Faruqi: No, it is not less kingly but the how of it needs to be specified. If you are saying that the king next started polishing the soldier's shoes and carrying his ordinance box, then this is not kingly. But remember that a Muslim believes that God is nearer to him than his jugular vein, and that our success is dependent upon Him. But to interpret this as a specific reduction of God's transcendence is not permissible.

Cragg: Reduction is not permissible certainly, but this is not reductionist. This is the whole point.

CHRISTIAN EXPERIENCE OF ISLAMIC DA'WAH,
WITH PARTICULAR REFERENCE TO AFRICA

LAMIN SANNEH

Lecturer in Islamics, University of Legon, Ghana

Christianity and Islam are united perhaps less by the things they have in common than by the things which divide them. It is true that both traditions teach doctrines of the virgin birth and of the messianic role of Jesus, among other things, and yet the Crusades took place when these things were common knowledge. On the reverse of the coin, the Muslim experience of the *Shari'ah* as the required standard of human obedience and duty towards God and towards each other is in contrast to the Christian teaching about the person of Christ or about the Eucharistic Mass. The risk of misunderstanding appears less in the things that separate the two sides then in the things which link them. Christian allegations that Islam is an imitation of Christianity are strongest in the similarities between the two, while Muslim claims that Islam has fulfilled and superceded Christianity are likely to be pressed hardest in areas of overlap. That one side or the other takes on such a role is more of a divisive than a uniting factor in our relationship. Even the fact that both religions claim a divine revelation can arouse separatist feelings or induce over-confidence, in either case blurring genuine lines of richness. The barriers which one attitude sets up, and the wide field of complacency created by the other, together make difficult mutual trust and real encounter.

Nevertheless certain methodological factors pose a common challenge and opportunity. For example, in the encounter with other religious traditions, our distinctive theological conceptions can be recognized alongside a desire for a common basis of approach and understanding. The missionary obligation of Islam and Christianity, to take an instance, could be approached not in terms of negative competitiveness or polite indifference but in terms of involvement and mutual exchange and sharing. Far from setting up harmful rivalry or congenial stalemate, both inevitable results of separation or over-confidence, the missionary ambitions of Islam and Christianity could, if properly understood, open new areas of dialogue, particularly at points where both are engaged in self-interpretation through the idiom of other cultures. By thus reflecting on the image of themselves projected by other peoples, Islam and Christianity may be able to come to grips with their hidden images.

I shall in the main body of this paper dwell at some length on the stimulus the African environment provided — and is still providing — for missionary Islam and how the resultant interaction constitutes a positive achievement for world Islam. My emphasis will be on Africans as missionary pioneers and spokesmen at royal courts and in towns and villages. In the concluding section I shall suggest how the Christian experience of Islamic religious activity could be a deepening and enriching experience. But a few general thoughts on bilateral co-operation between the two may be appropriate at this stage.

(1) **Christian teaching about the cross and the divinity of Christ on the one hand, and, on the other, Islamic teaching about the Qur'ānic revelation and the Divine Law (*Sharī'ah*) show a fundamental contrast of religious conception.** The Christian, starting with the great affirmations of faith in Christ and his work, is challenged to take seriously also the human aspects of Jesus' life by the Muslim insistence on his essential mortality. By contrast, the Muslim, furnished with a vast corpus on the Prophet's earthly life, might, under Christian stimulus, want to discover the *Logos* motif in Islam's history. Christians might try to look at the cross as an event in time through the resurrection miracle as an event beyond time, while Muslims in turn might wish to secure the miraculous basis of the Prophet's career alongside his concrete earthly achievements. With both our roots in time and eternity we could broaden each other's horizon by the mere fact of proceeding from our respective elevations. That is bound to be as stimulating as the discovery of common ground once promised.

(2) **A similar phenomenon of contrast also characterizes our attitude and response to the evangelical demands of witness and service.** While recognizing the value of each believer's obligation to be an instrument of conversion which is really God's work, both religions have assigned the task to a group of professional specialists living and working in society. Yet, the motivation and source of missionary activity derive from different conceptions and experience. The call to repentance is common to both religions, but in Islam the end and goal of religious conversion is acceptance of the unity of God and of Muhammad as his final if not his only envoy, with the consequent submission to the religious law, to which it is not permissible to add nor from which to subtract, at least in theory. In Christianity, by contrast, conversion results from accepting by faith the lordship of Jesus Christ as God's unique revelation and affiliating to a Church organized in his name. This affects also our views of how or where we encounter God, if at all, in the imperfect world of human beings. This prompts a question which is best taken up in the concluding section of the paper, namely, have Christians anything to learn from the Muslim version of faith and witness, and if so, can this help illuminate our common search for wholeness of which the Christian may have a particular understanding?

(3) **In the encounter between Islam — or Christianity — with Africa, several assumptions have been made which need to be briefly examined and evaluated.** One of the most widespread assumptions about Islam and Christianity in Africa is that, as foreign religions, both denigrated and devalued the African culture they neither understood nor respected. This attitude is most evident with regard to Christianity in Africa, but it is also true of Islam. I have elsewhere tried to answer this position as far as Islam is concerned, but it is so pervasive that a few more words seem necessary.

First of all, it seems to me not a disadvantage that such criticism was made, for where would Islam and Christianity themselves be if they had never been

53

attacked and condemned by opponents! But more seriously the proponents of easy and unfair missionary conquest seem curiously to be themselves under-rating the acute religious sense of the African and to be unheedful of the richly documented cases of communities who actively resisted or successfully adapted the incoming religion.

Secondly, it is a wild caricature of the indigenous religions to say that they melted away under fire of Muslim or Christian criticism because of an implicit lack of an inner religious or theological core. The tenacity with which these indigenous religions have continued to exercise a grip on African populations is proof that the early missionaries were not fighting an imagined or easy battle and that their well-deserved successes were often protracted and less often sure.

The third point is more fundamental than the preceding two. It is assumed, correctly, that the missionary religious scene in Africa is occupied by two major categories of people: the people who bring in the religion as transmitters and the people who embrace it as recipients. It is further assumed, this time incorrectly, that the more dominant of the two categories are the transmitters while the recipients play a more passive role in adopting what is introduced. Allegedly lacking in critical religious judgement, the recipients succumbed to the twin pressures of force and persuasion and even facilitated the attack on local religious customs. Hence the popularity with which many educated Africans today, following Western social anthropologists, have answered the call for "indigenization" and Africanization, two essentially distinct processes. But once we reverse the order and allow for the fact that Africans as recipients exercised a far more important role than the agents of transmission, it will undoubtedly take the patriotic thunder out of the discussion but it will also, more importantly, restore a much neglected historical perspective to the theme. Indigenization becomes the complex orientation of African populations as a continuous process rather than a determined phase coming after a period of so-called missionary subjugation.

One consequence of looking at the African as the more central of the two main classes of people is that the stress which mediaeval Arabic sources placed on the foreign trader as the pioneer of Islam would seem to be exaggerated. Whatever the connection between commerce and Islam, it is certainly less precise than we have been led to believe. Sir Thomas Arnold did us yeoman service when he detached Islam from the yoke of the sword and linked its preaching power to the short and long-range exploits of the trader. (See his *The Preaching of Islam*, London 1896, repr. Lahore 1967.) We need to travel further along the same road and separate Islam from theories of economic determinism and other causal explanations. What this leaves is Islam as a phenomenon with its own inner life and outwards modes of behaviour and manifestations.

One of the earliest pieces of tangible evidence for the conversion of Africans to Islam comes from the account of al-Bakri, writing in 1067 A.D. He says

54

that the ruler of ancient Mali turned to a Muslim cleric for help after a catastrophic drought descended on his land. The king had first tried in vain pagan religious options. As a precondition to attending to his request, the cleric required him to undergo Muslim catechism and embrace Islam, which he did. Then he and his Muslim patron undertook what is normally the prayer ritual for rain, *salāt al-istisqā*, and the following day, in answer to prayer, dramatic rain clouds developed and filled the heavens. The pagan priests, having been exposed by their failure to bring rain, lost their privileges and were banished by the king, their shrines desacralized. Al-Bakri adds that numerous people, many of them substantial citizens, followed the king's lead and embraced Islam.[1]

There is nothing in this story of an easy or simple triumphalist conquest by Islam. In a situation of genuine stalemate, Islam had to wait for its turn which came after pagan options had been tried without effect. The fact that pagan worship was not dismantled before Islam had proved its efficacy suggests that old religious attitudes persisted beyond the point of outward adherence to Islam.

My second example, relating to a twelfth century incident, comes from the seventeenth century chronicle, the *Ta'rīkh al-Sūdān*, by 'Abd al-Rahmān al-Sa'di. The ruler of the ancient Sudanic city of Jenne, Kanbara, decided one day to embrace Islam. He summoned in his presence all the leading scholars of the city, numbering above 4,200. In their midst he relinquished paganism and adopted Islam, and, almost as a bargain, promptly put three requests before them. Firstly, that any one coming to Jenne to seek refuge might find in the city ease and abundance and might as a consequence forget his former country. Secondly, that foreigners might flock into Jenne as their home and their numbers would outstrip the original inhabitants. Finally, that merchants travelling to the city might lose patience with conditions prevailing there and, anxious to leave it, might be compelled to dispose of their merchandise at derisory prices, to the benefit of the inhabitants.

The difficulty of this three-fold request might be seen, not so much in its range of demands as in how the first and the last could be reconciled to effect. The congregation concluded the meeting with a recitation of the *Fātihah* as a prayer seal. The chronicler was in no doubt that the requests were granted, his own patriotic faith standing him in good stead. Following this public conversion of the king and as a sign of his good faith his royal palace (*dār al-sultānah*), perhaps the *locus* of the imperial cult, was demolished and a community mosque raised on the site. A second edifice, most probably the residence of the new religious functionaries, was constructed adjacent to the mosque.[2]

1 Al-Bakri: *Kitāb al-masālik wa al-mamālik*, tr. and ed. M. G. de Slane (Alger 1913), repr. Paris 1965, text 74 ff., tr. 178 f.
2 *Ta'rīkh al-Sūdān*, tr. and ed. by Octave Houdas Paris 1964 (originally published 1913-1914), text 12-14, tr. 23-24.

It is clear in this account that Islam had long been in contention with pagan worship, and so was establishing its sway over well-charted religious territory. Instead of creating a fresh power base, it merely occupied the space and status vacated by its rival. What part internal or material factors played in the disintegration of the old religion is a matter for debate, but that Islam arrived on the scene quietly, without the drama of military confrontation, is self-evident. Indeed, the prayer technique employed to confirm Islam in the city is a replica of the role pagan worship had played. Like the account of al-Bakri, al-Sa'di's story has been unjustifiably used to support an economically motivated expansion of Islam in Jenne while the obvious position of the local clerics has been suppressed or explained away. But a recognition of the missionary significance of local clerics and other Muslim holy men in the dissemination of Islam will restore the long overdue pride of place to the recipients of religious influence. It will in the process also overturn the accepted commercial caveat of economic determinists.

A third example, still on Islamic influence on rulers, comes from ancient Mali and is given by Mahmūd al-Ka'ti in his book, the *Ta'rīkh al-Fattāsh*. The local Muslim clerics founded a settlement on the Bafing River called Diakhaba which acquired an immense stature as a clerical missionary centre, dedicated exclusively to the spread and practice of Islam. So powerful was this clerical tradition that the ruler of Mali was banned from entering it except once a year, on the 27th Ramadan when, as the deferential guest of the *qādī*, the chief judge and also the city's highest official, the king undertakes certain religious obligations. He arranges for meal offerings to be prepared. He places these in a large bowl which he carries on his head. Calling together Qur'ān students and little boys, he distributed the food from his head in a standing position. After consuming the food, the pupils call down blessings on the king as a concluding act. The *Ta'rīkh al-Fattāsh* says that Diakhaba ('Ja'ba') remained a redoubtable clerical strongold so that even those who were guilty of acts of hostility against the king could claim inviolable sanctuary within its borders. It continues: "they gave it the epithet, 'the city of God — *yaqāl lahu balad Allāh*' ".[3]

Although clearly possessing extraordinary authority as a religious missionary centre, Diakhaba was by no means untypical. A similar arrangement existed in Gunjūr, another clerical centre founded by emigrants from Diakhaba. There also power was exercised by the *qādī*, to whom the ruler, residing in a different place, paid his respects in his annual religious retreat to the centre. Both places were founded by a West African clerical clan, the Jakhanké.[4]

This account of the *Ta'rīkh al-Fattāsh* introduces many novel features about clerical Islam which need not detain us here. Some obvious parallels with

---

[3] *Ta'rīkh al-Fattāsh*, tr. and ed. by M. Delafosse and O. Houdas (1913-1914), Paris 1964, text 179, tr. 314.
[4] See author's article: "The Origins of Clericalism in West African Islam", *Journal of African History*, XVII, 1 (1976), 49-72.

the preceding examples stand out: trade and war seem to play an insignificant role in all the accounts. Also the role of Africans as recipients and missionary agents of Islam is underlined. Finally, Islam appears as a less self-confident religion, pursuing a course parallel with pagan worship which it is able sufficiently to undermine from within and eventually to replace. That a ruler takes on the mien of a humble pilgrim and, in an unroyal balancing posture, looks to the prayers of young innocents for his earthly and heavenly security smacks too much of local genius to need foreign stimulus. The original model for this practice must be lodged deep in the bosom of the African religious environment.

Another example, also from the *Ta'rīkh al-Fattāsh*, spotlights the importance of the cleric vis-à-vis the ruler. The present example improves on earlier ones by giving the cleric the upper hand in a confrontation with the ruler. After many attempts to assert his authority over Timbuktoo, the Askiya Muhammad Turé, king of Songhay, visits the city in person and summons the *qādī*, Mahmūd b. 'Umar, to an audience. In the ensuing discussion the *askiya* demanded to know why the *qādī* had resisted his orders and turned away his message-bearers. After a flurry of short questions and answers between the two of them, the *qādī* explained his conduct in these words:

> Have you forgotten, or are you feigning ignorance, how one day you came to my house and, crawling up to me, you took me by the feet and held on to my garments and said, "I have come so that you may place yourself in safety between me and the fire of damnation. Help me and hold me by the hand lest I stumble into hell fire. I entrust myself in safekeeping to you." It is for this reason that I have chased away your message-bearers and resisted your commands.[5]

A remarkable position with which the king, more remarkably still, unreservedly concurred. He declared in turn:

> By God, it is true that I have forgotten this, but you have now reminded me and you are absolutely right. By God, you deserve great reward for you have saved me from harm. May God exalt your rank and make you my security against the fire. What I have done has provoked the wrath of the All-Powerful, but I beg His forgiveness and turn in penitence to Him. In spite of what I have done I still invoke your protection and attach myself to you. Confirm me in this position under you and God will confirm you (and through you) defend me.[6]

It is just possible that the chronicler may in this passage be attempting to paint an exaggeratedly pious image of the *askiya*, but if so then he is employing a device which shows his royal patron being challenged with impunity by a subordinate official. Unless the story is true, the king stands more to lose by it than to benefit from it. That such an encounter took place I think we can safely accept. It shows, among other things, the esteem in which religion is held by Africans, king and commoner alike. It also demonstrates a profound participation in the religious and moral quest.

---

5 *Ta'rīkh al-Fattāsh*, text 60-61, tr. 116-117.
6 *Ibid.*, text 61, tr. 117.

Thus far we have witnessed one method of propagating Islam, namely, the peaceful way which places emphasis on strengthening Islam from within, a process of revitalization to which the name *tajdīd* is given. We shall return to it later, but another important method of Islamic expansion is through the adoption of military measures in a *jihād*. This is the more dramatic but certainly less frequent device of maintaining Islam's missionary strength. Yet even in *jihāds* there was great concern that weak Muslims should be enabled to escape falling deeper into grave error, and sometimes this concern was paramount over the desire for conquest and booty.

In this sense one of the greatest missionary movements in African Islam was that led by the Fulani, 'Uthmān dan Fodio and his lieutenants. Beginning about 1786 until his death in 1817, the Shehu, as he came to be known, toured widely in the Hausa states of North Nigeria preaching Islam and extending the frontiers of his authority. He established the caliphate during this time, with the capital at Sokoto, although he himself withdrew from active politics and allowed his son and brother, Muhammad Bello and 'Abd Allāh dan Fodio, to take the reins of power. Like other Muslim clerics, the Shehu confronted local political rulers with demands and requests which were mostly granted. For example, he required, and obtained, the submission to Islam of the vacillating sultan of Gobir, Bawa. The latter also bowed to the Shehu's request to free the ruler of a neighbouring state with which Gobir was at loggerheads. In fact the Shehu counselled Bawa during some of the sultan's more difficult military campaigns, and a local chronicle says that Bawa lost his life (1790) in an operation in which he foolhardily exceeded the limits the Shehu had set up.[7]

The Shehu as an individual is outstanding, but he is neither unique nor representative of the broad pattern of islamization and missionary expansion. Many individuals stood in the same militant tradition, devout men who unsheathed the sword of righteousness against unbelief and charlatanry. As one writer observes, while it is true that Islam took on the colour of water in many societies, it is also true that in others "it is dyed with blood". The *jihād* was adopted as a stern and irrevocable duty against polytheists and those venal *malams* (scholars) who encouraged *détente* with unjust rulers. The jihadists were particularly scathing towards such Muslim scholars who had compromised the faith, misled unwary Muslims and titillated the fancy of oppressive rulers, all this on the basis of bogus credentials![8]

The Shehu is also unrepresentative of the broad pattern of islamization. Recent research, in which the present writer has had a share, has revealed the existence in West Africa of a strong clerical clan with a long history of missionary endeavour, with a pacific and politically neutral reputation to boot.

---

[7] Mervyn Hiskett: *The Sword of Truth: the life & times of Shehu Usuman dan Fodio* (New York: Oxford University Press 1973, 42-46).
[8] Mervyn Hiskett: "The Islamic Tradition of Reform in the Western Sudan from the 16th to the 18th century", *Bulletin of the School of Oriental & African Studies*, XXV, 3 (1962), 575-596.

The tantalizing references to Islam in ancient Ghana and Mali, with particular reference to the Serakhulle (usually called Soninké) inhabitants of Ghana, can now be more meaningfully gathered together, though that is best done elsewhere. The Serakhulle clerics are the most powerful and enduring group in Black African Islam. Better known as the Jakhanké ('Diakhanke' in French sources) they trace their origin to a 12th century Muslim figure, al-Hājj Salim Suwaré. The Jakhanké clerics, who founded Diakhaba and Gunjur already referred to, established a missionary career based on a scrupulous avoidance of war and politics (al-harb wa al-siyāsah), including chieftaincy office for themselves. In modern times they created a prosperous centre at Touba in Guinea (1803). The town was invaded and occupied without opposition by the French in 1911. The present Maliki muftī of Senegal and the muftī of Haute Volta are both of Jakhanké stock. The Jakhanke are reputed to have spread Islam to Hausaland in the fifteenth century and today they or their disciples can be found in various parts of Africa. Characteristic of their mode of expansion is the creation of what they call a majlis, essentially a clerical/educational parish from which Islam is taken to surrounding areas. Names for such majlis centres sometimes suggest their missionary purpose: Nibrās (lantern light), Touba (blessedness, tree of Paradise), Taybatu (sweet-smelling, an epithet for Madina), Nema (ni'mah, grace, blessing), Dār Salām (abode of peace, sphere of Islam), and so on.

In the same peaceful, if controversial vein could be fitted the Ahmadiyah Muslim missionary movement in many parts of West Africa. The Ahmadis have been very warily received, if not repudiated, by Sunni Muslim communities in West Africa,[9] and their inclusion here is only for the purpose of emphasizing that even in a distant tributary of Islam the missionary ardour was far from being quenched. Their involvement in modern schools and medical care is an example of Muslim awareness of opportunities for service, just as Christians discovered in their pioneer years.

It remains now to consider, in this final section, how Christians could understand and respond to such Islamic missionary activity. This is best done by outlining first the stages through which our relations with Muslims have gone.

There was, first, the era of great rivalry. Christians and Muslims regarded each other with something bordering on hysteria as each side billeted recruits to wage its campaign. The Christian missionary movement, in so far as it was controlled by outside bodies, found itself sharing aims with the colonial administration in certain places. One aim in which both co-operated was the attempt to check the spread of Islam as an anti-Christian and an anti-colonial

---

[9] Al-Hajj Muhammad Fādilu Fadera, of Senegambia, has strongly condemned the Ahmadiyah in a closely written 45-page booklet: Kitāb Tahdhīru Ummati 'l-Muhammadiyāti min Ittibāʻi 'l-firqati Ahmadīyati (A Warning to the Muslim Community on the dangers of following the Ahmadiyah Sect). Printed in Dakar (n.d.). During field-work in 1972 the present writer saw evidence of the document being disseminated along travel routes.

force. The missionaries were also acting from fear, fear of losing African converts to Islam. It was a similar motive which led some later missionaries to acquiesce grudgingly in the apparent ease with which Islam was gaining adherents. Gradually Christian missionaries came to acquire a reserved tolerance for Islam on the grounds that it established a tender bridge to a higher revelation which the African was incapable of reaching in one brief stride. A paradox developed here: the call to Christian service must be obeyed towards Africans for whom the claims of a rival religion were admitted to be more suitable! The other side of the paradox cut against the Church which laboured under a self-inflicted pessimism in the face of alleged Islamic expansion in Africa. And yet the picture it painted, or allowed to be painted, of Islamic strength in Africa and of its own not inconsiderable contribution to the missionary enterprise concealed the true nature of the process of religious change in the two religions. It also paved the way for a vocal, but by no means representative, reaction to Christianity as a religion imposed institutionally from outside, thus reinforcing the now questionable supposition that the transmitters of the faith were in a superior position over the recipients.

The era of rivalry had its colonial version too. The French, perhaps more than the British, Portuguese or Germans, were deeply involved with Islam in North and West Africa. At one stage so resolved were the French to scotch what they alarmingly called "the Islamic peril" that they staged what a French scholar/administrator termed "the St. Bartholomew's massacre of the marabouts".[10] In fact this was mainly a round-up operation of the leading Muslim scholars of Guinea precedent to their incarceration in Mauritania. This was the incident described above when the French invaded Touba in 1911 and arrested the leading Jakhanké clerics along with others on suspicion of fomenting a maraboutic insurrection. It was clear that the French were acting upon an articulate policy toward Islam. For example, a French officer serving in the Algerian colonial service was once dispatched to West Africa with specific orders to report on the most effective means to be employed to halt the march of Islam in lands slowly coming under French protection. Particularly the French wanted to know the feasibility of a *cordon sanitaire* being set up in Islam's path. All these efforts were ironically facilitated by the propensity of African Muslims to withdraw into obscure enclaves to practise the faith.

One of the best examples of the coalescence of such Christian missionary fear of Islam and colonial mistrust was Freetown where, in the mid-nineteenth century, a policy was evolved to try to check the flow of Muslims from the hinterland into the Freetown peninsula, and once there to segregate the two groups in demarcated residential areas. This was called the Parish Scheme. But a short time later the situation was dramatically altered, chiefly as a result of the single-handed efforts of Dr Edward Blyden, the great Black nationalist.[11]

---

[10] Paul Marty: *L'Islam en Guinée* (Paris 1921), 117. See also Mourey and Terrier: *L'Expansion Française et la Formation Territoriale* (Paris 1910), 234.
[11] Dr Blyden's formative work was on this subject: *Christianity, Islam and the Negro Race* (London 1887), repr. Edinburgh 1967.

The era of rivalry between the two religions was followed by what we may loosely term "the years of confinement". Islam's retreat before encroaching colonialism had reached an advanced stage by the time strong local Christian communities were established, and the two sides remained in comparative isolation. The one nestled along the coast, nurtured by a strong commercial population, while the other pined in rustic cloisters. Walter Miller, for example, the pioneer missionary of the Church Missionary Society in North Nigeria, observed censoriously that the Muslim leaders believed that "their isolation from the world was almost hermetic, and only the merest breath of information stole through the few, not quite closed doors".[12] But even Muslims in full retreat were asking if the period of isolation looming ahead need be an inevitable or permanent stalemate. One European pioneer was asked by a group of keen Muslims: "Why dost thou not respect our prophet as an envoy from the Most High, since we acknowledge Christ as such?"[13]

This era of confinement was to have disastrous effect on the work of Christian bridge-builders like Dr Blyden whose attempts to establish modern schools among Muslims, with the necessary government support, were resisted by Muslim isolationists like Legally Savage. While it is true that Christians have unwarrantedly feared or, in isolation, misrepresented the strengths and weaknesses of Islam, it is also true, almost as a necessary corollary, that Muslims have had like perception of Christians.

The apparent failure, however, of people like Dr Blyden or Legally Savage points a real need for both communities to emerge from confinement and isolation. The retreat which imperial rule precipitated among Muslims was extended by the emergence of nationalist politics and independence. The relative inability of traditional Muslim élites to compete successfully for jobs in modern states has robbed them further of many of those ideals which prompted their withdrawal. The phenomenon of Muslim constituents, under the direction of the traditional 'ulamā (scholars), voting into power men with whom they share little or no confessional solidarity is a demonstration of the withdrawal attitude. This only postpones some of the issues which confinement has created.

A partial withdrawal, which relies on the amenability of local politicians to Muslim demands and interests, could prepare the way for loosening the chains of confinement. Muslim interests might be seen to lie more and more in the arena of modern options, as numerous groups and organizations in Freetown and elsewhere are discovering, and with such a gradual shift of the centre of Muslim activity there might come an increase in Christian contact already under way in many places.

---

12 Walter Miller: *Reflections of a Pioneer* (London 1936), 23. Miller was writing in about 1900.
13 Gaspard Mollien: *Travels in Africa to the Sources of the Senegal and Gambia in 1818* (London 1820), 51.

The rise and growth of Independency in the African Christian church, is a movement of reform and renewal similar in many ways to the *jihād* movement in Islam. Historians concerned only with the political basis of African Christianity have stressed the anti-élitist position of Independency. However, Independency has made striking use of apocalyptic materials from the Bible and combined these with a messianic creed. Organizationally, it has relied on charismatic concepts of authority vested in the founder's family. Both Independency and the *jihād* strove after a millenarian version of religion, with an apocalyptic anticipation of divine intervention and triumph in human affairs. Both used dreams and visions to supplement standard revelation. Both denounced the leadership under which they had once lived. Both made membership of their movement a prerequisite of sound faith. Both encouraged withdrawal from the world and both used the office of prophecy to proclaim the impending arrival of God's reign. Until that happened, and to help hasten its coming, both Independency and the *jihād* riveted on their followers the heavy chains of discipline and personal sacrifice. To emphasize their break with, and disdain of, the world, both movements employed divinatory techniques of obtaining guidance and giving instructions and orders to secure allegiance. Finally, in heralding the coming of the expected millenium, both preached a triumphalist message in which their version of sin and injustice determined where and against whom the sword of truth was to be wielded. The *jihād*, of course, combined physical combat with spiritual warfare, whereas Independency contented itself with waging only a spiritual struggle.

Thus the emergence of Independency has reminded other Christians of the vigorous field of interaction which exists between the church and the African context in which it is situated. Hence the renewed interest in the church in customary religious practices in Africa. A new field of dialogue has been discovered almost within the walls of the church. A similar situation has always existed in Islam. One brief example may suffice. Local accounts say that when Islam was first introduced to Yorubaland (perhaps in the eleventh or twelfth century) by a Hausa Muslim, the people of Ife at first resisted the new faith, but afterward retrieved the sack of the missionary containing a copy of the Qur'ān, covered it with a pot and began to worship it as Odudua. Thus began the cult of Odudua among the Yorubas.[14] Of course this is only a story and may not actually describe an historical incident. But it does show how Islam can be conceived among traditional worshippers, namely, as a stimulus and articulator.

The field of dialogue which Independency has widened is one which the churches in Africa have recently begun to explore. In 1960 it was agreed to institutionalize this concern for dialogue with Islam, and thus was created the Islam-in-Africa Project. It grew out of the concern of the Churches to train their people more so that they can carry out their responsibility towards their Muslim neighbours and interpret faithfully the Gospel of Jesus Christ.

---

14 R. E. Dennett: *Nigerian Studies* (London 1910), 75. Dennett reproduces a local account.

Christians ill-informed or ill-motivated may be unable to witness meaningfully to the Gospel, and their neighbourliness with Muslims may be impoverished or distorted. It is in the interest of both sides that a strong, confident witness by the church be seen to be grounded in right understanding. For example, Muslims are known to have complained about the this-worldly preoccupation of many Christians and to have wished for more evident concern with theological matters. The fact that we are both involved in creative tension with the pagan religious traditions of Africa is reason enough for us to compare and exchange views as a matter of practical urgency. Signs are hopeful, for much of what the I.A.P. produces as literature has been in almost equal demand by Muslims and Christians: factual accounts of the two religions, the challenge of identification with the non-literate pagan religions of Africa, and imaginative, sympathetic descriptions of the spiritual life. Public meetings, lectures and talks, drawing both Muslims and Christians, have also been in demand.

The I.A.P. then, as a modest contribution of the churches in Africa to bilateral harmony between the two faiths, has clearly filled a need. In this sense it has also helped prepare the way for the next stage in our relationship, i.e., encounter. The confident, though conciliatory, approach that the I.A.P. has shaped and encouraged in dialogue is itself a contributory factor to genuine encounter. It would be unflattering to Islam to suggest that it can be encountered only when the full claims of Christianity are mitigated by a desire for a temporary or illusory solidarity. To demand the removal of boundaries as a precondition to meeting is to deny its possibility. True friendship can extend those boundaries into bonds of unity.

If a question is asked about the Christian's experience of Islamic religious activity, three things need to be said. The first is that the Christian recognizes immediately the religious stature and integrity of Islam and the way the African setting seems to have accentuated the theological and moral aspects of the faith. The devout and humble clerics held emperors, kings and princes to account through the clerics' frail grasp and partial glimpse of the Creator. There is of course a danger that religion can be set up as a consolidated power structure and deified or demonized. But that danger is not avoided by trying to "reduce" religion to functional or utilitarian forms. The Christian is encouraged by the frank and direct way Islam appears to have understood and discharged its missionary obligation.

The second thing to say is that in spite of the close identity of Islam and the African religious scene, there was a fundamental unity of thought and practice with world Islam. The Arabic language of the Qur'ān and the commentaries, the prayer postures, the Islamic lunar calendar and the figure and example of the Prophet have all helped strengthen the universal missionary appeal of Islam. The Christian could derive ecumenical profit from this confessional solidarity of Islam.

A third observation relates to religious triumphalism which both Christians and Muslims have separately espoused. Although triumphalist movements have dramatized legitimate objections to this world as the ultimate and absolute, there are nevertheless some pitfalls. But first a word about motives. It is right that religious people should feel impatient with an unjust, oppressive and callous social and political order. The stark dichotomy between a world deeply scarred by cruelty, exploitation and poverty on the one hand, and, on the other, a vision of another, unsullied and radiant through God's righteous presence, is enough to stir people of conscience in the deepest recesses of their sense of duty and loyalty. That is the stuff of which the Psalms are made.

Nevertheless there can be difficulties. Religious programmes designed to remedy such an inadequate world have failed in their turn. An elevated vision of the Kingdom of God is no guarantee of its realization, nor of the means to it, and the records of both Muslims and Christians are littered with the broken hopes of religious idealists. The question asked above may now be taken up again: to what extent can we as religious people hold firmly to the promise of the kingdom to come and still participate meaningfully, if critically, in an imperfect world? If we have made a fetish of success in the past, and reaped retributive failure in consequence, are we not in equal danger today of idolizing mediocrity and indifference?

Three things to say on this. First, Christians have learnt — and are learning — to assimilate into their thinking and life an uneven missionary record. The call to evangelical obedience to Jesus Christ has not always been answered faithfully, or consistently.

Second, Christian experience of Islamic *da'wah* in Africa can be both stimulating and challenging. It is stimulating because it has shown Christians how seriously the vocation to witness needs to be taken. The devotion and sense of self-sacrifice which Muslims have shown in obedience to the call to spread and establish the faith are a poignant reminder of what lies at the heart of Christian discipleship. Almost from their earliest contact with Muslim groups, Christian observers have written admiringly of the public practice of Islam. The muezzin's brisk and clear call to prayer, the simple daily gestures of surrender and self-abasement before the Creator in the prayer ritual, and the donning of the garb of poverty, self-denial and personal sacrifice in the fast of Ramadan are some of the things specially noted. Even a well-seasoned Muslim traveller like Ibn Battūta was astonished in 1352 A.D. when he saw the esteem in which local Muslims in West Africa held Qur'ānic learning, and their punctillious observance of Friday worship made an equally favourable impression on him.[15] The challenge consists in learning through commitment an identical lesson of humility. The Muslim reformers discovered fairly quickly that their confidence in the supremacy of the revealed law had to be tempered with the experience of people's ambivalence or weakness even when they professed the creed, thus suggesting that the path to absolute submission is a difficult and often elusive one.

---

15 Ibn Battūta: *Travels in Asia and Africa*, tr. and ed. H. A. R. Gibb (London 1929), repr. 1957, 330.

The third and final point, arising out of the preceding one, is that Islam's successes made it vulnerable to men with worldly ambition and schismatic consequences followed. The community of the faithful, spread over vast lands of wealth and power, succumbed to internal dissension and factionalism. Rebellions broke up the unity forged in the fire of faith and reform. All this is a reminder to Christians as well that this world cannot be a substitute for the true reign of God. The broken records of our attempts, the broken vessels of human communication by which we have sought to transmit the message of God's loving mercy, this brokenness is encountered for the Christian in the broken body of Christ. The stumbling steps we take and the stammering words of response we mumble to the divine *daʿwah* are not a charge against us, thanks to the Lord's utter brokenness. The Christian recognizes that human failure, particularly in things of the spirit, however, devastating, does not ultimately condemn us to futility, for that would be surrendering to the world what truly belongs to God. Rather, the ambivalent chaos and order out of which we have sought wholeness exist under his judgement, and that judgement has been executed in Christ's brokenness. Thus while we may not blasphemously deify the world in which chaos and order coexist, we are nevertheless encouraged to rejoice in it because the brokenness of Christ has consecrated it for the witness and service of those seeking wholeness. Thus to hope for the fulfilment of the kingdom in a world as imperfect as ours is not an escapist solution but an essential condition of discovering the truth about our hope for ultimate wholeness through Christ's brokenness. The early Christians celebrated Christ's sacrifice in the context of anticipating God's true reign. Such openness towards the future and the belief that it is not our blueprints that will secure God's inevitable vindication of our particular cause justify the Christian's experience of trembling hope in an imperfect world.

﷽﷽﷽﷽﷽﷽﷽﷽﷽﷽﷽﷽﷽﷽﷽﷽﷽﷽﷽﷽﷽﷽﷽﷽﷽﷽﷽

Several participants remarked on the ecumenical spirit of Dr Sanneh's presentation, its unpolemic tone. Did this reflect a basic tolerance inherent in the African situation? These remarks led Dr Sanneh to make some further observations about the African situation with regard to African family life. (Editors)

Sanneh: A fairly unique aspect of African religiosity is the fact that in the African family we are likely to find various religions represented by different members of the family living in the same house. The father may be a Muslim, the uncle a Christian; one son may go to a Muslim school, another to a Christian school, and so on. Now while this situation may have inherent dangers, I think it also throws up many challenges which, if faced, could lead to the health of our respective traditions. I believe the African family is saying something to the West about inter-religious encounter which might help to relate Christians and Muslims to each other in society at large. The tendency in the West seems to be to operate from the competitive tensions of the wider society which are then introduced conceptually into the family. In the African setting I have the feeling that we have to start the other way round, and come to talk about society from the point of view of the family. The family in Africa is the solvent of religious tensions existing within the wider society.

Rudvin: I think this is a very important point, not least, as you suggest, for the developing situation in the West. But you said that the African family situation may have certain inherent dangers. What do you have in mind?

Sanneh: The problem is to try to safeguard the separate integrity of Islam and Christianity as represented in the African family, so that neither religion degenerates into a kind of lethargic syncretism, in which religious ideas are compared, not on the basis of the genuine challenge which the religions represent, but in terms of just getting on and avoiding any distinctive responsibility. With the two religions meeting in daily and intimate contact within the family it's easy for us to think, "There are no real differences", and the door is shut to any kind of enquiry into the separate credentials of Islam and Christianity; dialogue is stifled and people who represent both Islam and Christianity in the family are not able to take full advantage of the enormous richness and resources offered by their respective religions. This is really our problem. In other words, we want to enter the genuine sphere of missionary encounter in which the representatives of the two religions take seriously their religious calling in their relations with others, whereas in the West, and in other parts of the world, I imagine that the task is really to restrain and to hold back, in Africa we need to stimulate and encourage.

Khurshid Ahmad then took up the issue of indigenization which Dr Sanneh had raised in his paper. (Editors)

Ahmad: Indigenization has not been a particular problem in the Islamic experience, because in Islam there is a built-in process through which indigenous elements are assimilated within the religious and social framework. What strikes me most is that these indigenous traditions are expressed in modes of behaviour which do not conflict with the values and ideals of Islam. They are made part of the total process of Islamization, and at the same time they are given a new direction, a new character. They no longer remain foreign elements but become part and parcel of the system. This is the creative part which Islamic tradition plays in accepting what is acceptable from the local tradition. This, I think, is something which deserves to be examined much more seriously, keeping in view the demands of peace and the growth of human society in a multi-religious and multi-cultural situation such as that towards which we are all moving. It would be a folly to think that juxtaposition of conflicting elements can enrich a tradition. Islam rejects what conflicts with its values and assimilates what can become a part of its system, more or less in the same way as the living human organism does to food it receives from without.

66

Sanneh: Let's be quite clear about one thing. Accounts describing the growth of Islam in Africa show that Islam gained adherents in Africa largely through the appeal of its teaching, the Arabic language as the vehicle of divine revelation of the Qur'ān, the *shahādah* of Islam, the *salāt* of Islam — this being the particularly distinctive element of Muslim activity by which Muslims came to be known, and by which they are still known, in many African languages as "the praying men". The desire for booty, the desire for economic gain and the military appeal of Islam were minor factors. *Jihād* as the active establishment of Islamic *da'wah* in Africa is a highly complex phenomenon. The people who were engaged in *jihād* were primarily concerned with the *jihād al-kabīr* — the greater *jihād*, which is spiritual struggle to purify the motives of Muslims living in the *dār al-Islām*, to renew the faith, to re-vitalize the spirit of Muslims and help to enable weak, syncretist and compromising Muslims to grasp the distinctive calling of Islam. This was really the primary interest of the jihadists. Even when military measures were adopted, they were adopted not to convert pagans to Islam but to protect the Muslim community and also Muslims living sometimes under pagan rule and sometimes in mixed situations. Their purpose was to protect them from being victimized. So far as Africa is concerned, *jihād* was accompanied by a vigorous process of strengthening and confirming Muslims within the Muslim community, the process which is called *tajdīd*.

This discussion led Dr Sanneh to comment further on another point in his paper of importance in respect of indigenization. (Editors)

Sanneh: As I've said, in the past almost everyone writing about the spread of both Islam and Christianity in Africa has assumed that the "transmitters" of these two religions, the missionaries, have been the dominant party over the "recipients" of the imported faiths, that's to say the indigenous Africans. And it is in these terms that the issue of indigenization is then considered. My own investigations have led me to the opposite conclusion: the more dominant of the two categories has in fact been the "recipients".

And since we are all enamoured of the secular mission of the West to under-developed parts of the world, let me use a mechanical example. A man bought a bicycle and was riding it in the Nigerian bush when he had a flat tyre. He could not mend his puncture. So he dismantled the wheel, removed the outer tube of the bicycle wheel and stuffed it with straw which he gathered from the bush; then he mounted the outer tube and rode on. It is clear here that no repair kit helped the man to adjust to the environment in which he received the bicycle, but rather it was the African setting — the abundance of grass and hay — and his own ability to adapt the bicycle to his needs which enabled him to improvise in that way. And this I believe is a parable of what really happened to the religious content of Islam and Christianity as they were received by the Africans. The African environment is an active, vitally dynamic field in which incoming religious influences are moulded by the African genius to suit African need. And this is as it should be. But if this is so, then the whole school of African religious historiography needs to be reviewed, because it means that we have missed somehow the vital significance of the African as the recipient of the religion. With all due respect for the heroic self-sacrifice of the missionary — Muslim and Christian — they have really occupied an inferior position in the religious scene in Africa.

Mr Ali Muhsin, speaking out of long experience of relations between Muslims and Christians in East Africa, gently drew the discussion toward more practical issues. (Editors)

Muhsin: I am particularly intrigued by the ecumenical spirit of Dr Sanneh's exposition as being fundamentally African. But it is also, I should say, characteristically Islamic. This, indeed, has been the history of Islam. Islam has been an absorbing religion rather than a converting one — this is the point Khurshid Ahmad was making earlier. Islam is the religion of nature, and those who have deviated from its straight path will sooner or later come back to it; like water finding its own level and all rivers flowing down to the endless ocean, so all concepts of faith will finally find their way to a common denominator.

However, we should not be idealistic dreamers but practical people and the practical reality is that there are believing and practising Christians and there are believing and practising Muslims. How should these two come together and co-operate at the present time? That is the problem, and that is the question which Dr Sanneh has asked in his paper. I personally believe that there is a great deal that can be done. The most important thing is that people should understand that we must live together, whether as a nation or as human beings. As a person who has had some experience in government, however short, and however fatal in its results, I think that when you get a minority — whether it is tribal or racial or religious — one must try one's level best not to make that minority feel a minority. Opportunities should be available for all, and not only opportunities. In many African countries we find that the government declares that there are equal opportunities for all, but the point is that the person who is handicapped must first be helped to overcome his handicap, and the historical past must be taken into consideration. Those that were backward must be helped to go forward. As much as possible must be done to correct imbalances. Otherwise the alternative is that which we see happening in Lebanon, in Northern Ireland, and what happened in Uganda, and what could happen in so many other countries. These are really serious things and must be tackled more seriously. And let us not forget the words of Samuel Coleridge who said: "He who begins by loving Christianity better than truth will proceed by loving his own sect or church better than Christianity, and by loving himself better than all." I think this should be said not only to Christians but also to Muslims.

CHRISTIAN MISSION IN THE MUSLIM WORLD

Two Case Studies

Dr Muhammad Rasjidi and Mr Ali Muhsin Barwani presented two papers on Muslim experience of Christian missions, focusing attention on two strategic areas, Indonesia and East Africa. As the two papers taken together along with the material presented in introducing the papers required much greater space than could be provided in this issue of the IRM, these papers had to be cut drastically to bring them to size. Dr Rasjidi was able to revise his paper in the light of discussions at the Conference. The final editing of these two papers has been done by Khurshid Ahmad. (Editors)

THE ROLE OF CHRISTIAN MISSIONS
THE INDONESIAN EXPERIENCE

MUHAMMAD RASJIDI

Professor of Islamics, University of Indonesia, Jakarta

If we look back to the period between World War I and World War II, we find that almost the entire Muslim world was under western influence, either directly as colonies or indirectly as protectorates or mandate countries. Although there were a few theoretical exceptions like Iran, Afghanistan and Turkey, they were equally exposed to Western colonial influences, political as well as cultural. This period will go down in history as a period of de-Islamization and secularization of the Muslim world.

A major characteristic of this period has been overt and covert introduction and even imposition of Christianity under the patronage of colonial powers or through their connivance. One of the important articles of the statutes of the East Indies Company, outlining the aims of the Company, stipulated that the spread of Christianity was one of the objectives to be pursued. Instructions of the Dutch Company contained the provision that the Governor General, Jean Pieterzon Coen, should supply the necessary means for spreading the Christian religion.

Although promotion of Christianity was one of the objectives of the colonial powers, it deserves to be said in fairness to them, that their most important objective was economic and political exploitation. This is evident in the fact that once their grip was complete on the Islamic countries, they started showing some accommodation on the religious front. The British gradually accepted the principle of respect for the religions and customs of the peoples of the Indo-Pakistan sub-continent. When the Dutch missionaries urged the Dutch Government to take steps on a large scale to Christianize the Indonesian people in 1870, the Government advisor, Snouck Hurgronje, rejected their demand and said that the Indonesians, especially those in Java, already had Islam as their religion. Nonetheless, the economic and political exploitation was carried on under the guise of beautiful slogans such as the "white man's burden" and "the civilizing mission", which in fact meant the imposition of Western culture on the Muslim East.

During the colonial period, missionaries firmly entrenched themselves in many Muslim countries. They built schools and hospitals, in addition to churches. In fact, education and health were two pressing needs of the peoples of the colonies. Missions were invited to penetrate through these most sensitive areas.

If we look at the role of the American University or the Jesuit College of St. Joseph in Beirut, we can understant how great and all-pervasive was the influence of these institutions on the minds of their students and how they succeeded in undermining the Islamic tradition in its own homeland.

Dr Leslie Newbigin says in his book *Honest Religion for Secular Man*: "Missionaries in India and Africa have been agents of secularization even if they did not realize it. Like the first Christians who refused obeissance either to the pagan gods or to the divine emperor and who were therefore denounced as atheists, their teaching and practice has the effect of disintegrating the sacral bonds that have traditionally held society together. Through their vast educational programme, they introduced into the minds of the younger generations ideas which were bound to call the old religious order into question. At an earlier period, the missionary in India would not have put it that way. He would admit probably that he intended and expected to replace the pagan society with a Christian one. His mission compounds, his Christian colonies and his magnificent apparatus of Christian schools, colleges, hospitals and farms were a preliminary sketch for that Indian christendom. He hoped to share with India the privileges of a Christian civilization."

I would like to underline the term "Christian civilization". It is an important example of misapplication of terms. Everyone knows that the present science and technology began in Western Europe. But is one justified in calling that science and technology "Christian"?

But after World War II, the situation changed. Every national government is now trying in its own way to educate people and provide them with medical care and other services. Although conditions differ from place to place, yet in general all developing countries are making great strides in education and health. Now, in 1976, missionaries are no longer the major agency for the promotion of education and the preservation of health. These tasks have been taken over, for the most part, by national governments.

Bishop Newbigin says "In the third place, there are the new nations of Asia and Africa, recently freed from the control of the European powers and seeking to develop a stable national life as independent entities. Here there is no background of Christendom except as it was represented in the mission compounds and the colonial chaplaincies. The major impact of the western world has been through education (much of it initiated by Christian missions), commercial and industrial development and through the impact of political ideas. The churches are small minorities, generally with little direct influence on the course of national life. While the power of the old religions is diminishing, they still have immense influence upon the way in which men think and act. The process of secularization is still, especially in the Islamic countries, in an early stage". (p. 125.)

As the question of secularization is crucial in our evaluation of the role of Christian Missions, let me state clearly that we as Muslims feel strongly that missionaries have, to a large extent, misunderstood Islam. In their opinion, everything in Islam is sacral. Christianity secularizes. In Islam man is not involved in this world; it is Christianity which made man involved in worldly affairs. Bible is a secular book, but not the Qur'ān. Islamic countries are still slow in secularization, and they can progress only if they secularize quickly. To a Muslim all this is either a product of ignorance of Islam and the ethos of the Muslim society or a clever way to undermine the foundations on which Muslim life and society are established. We achieve this worldliness within the framework of Islam and any attempt to impose a secularization that destroys the Islamic framework is, to us, a mad rush to chaos and destruction.

The Indonesian Situation Today

This is the background against which present efforts to develop dialogue between Christianity and Islam are being made. These efforts are important, but they can bear fruit only if we can put an end to the gross abuse of services and institutions in the hands of the Christian missions at work in the world of Islam. This plagues the relationships between the two religious communities. I would like to describe frankly to you what I see every day in Indonesia.[1]

Exploiting the economic and political situation in Indonesia, Christian missionaries are doing such things as the following:

1. Churches are being built in the midst of Muslim villages and rice fields, and in strategic corners of big towns, out of all proportion to the Christian presence in the area. Missionaries are purchasing strategically situated lands at sky-high prices in order to build churches and schools. If the proprietor of the desired land shows unwillingness to sell it, missionaries send neutral persons who purchase the land in their own name but a little later sell it to the missionaries.

---

[1] For a valuable contribution from a Christian scholar on the outlines of a code of ethics for missionary behaviour, see Daniel J. Fleming: "A Code of Ethics" in *Relations Among Religious Today* (Leiden: Brill, 1963).

71

2. The church distributes rice, clothes and money among the poor people and uses these things to bring them closer to their mission. The church lends money or natural manures and seeds to impoverished peasants on condition that they send their children to missionary schools. Mission gives fellowships to good students, undergraduates as well as post-graduates. There is a foundation called "Students' Crusade" to take care of this part of the invasion. In South Kalimah a foundation financed by West Germany is engaged in providing food and financing schools.

3. Immediately after the communist insurgency in 1965, members of the outlawed communist party who were detained in jails were approached by missionary agents; those agents promised to supply rice and cash to their families on condition that they sign a paper declaring that they have been converted to Christianity. Communists used this opportunity to gain a Christian label and have ever since used this cover for their activities.

4. Missionary institutions have introduced a "Foster Parents" system for students of high schools and primary schools. They provide school fees, pocket money, books and even clothes through the foster fathers who are in Australia, Canada and America. These foster fathers maintain correspondence with their foster children especially at Christian holidays and on religious occasions like Christmas, Easter, etc. On those occasions they send special gifts. This has been a very clever way of influencing the minds and feelings of these children. The foster father system has had much success in Jogjakarta and Bali and has led to conversions.

5. Christian girls try to convert Muslim youth by resorting to unbecoming means. Christian youth are trying to convert Muslim girls. There is a lot of covert use of sex in bringing the younger generation of Islam closer to Christianity. Instances of this are appearing in the Muslim press.

6. Christian youth persuade Muslim minors to go to movies and places of recreation, giving them sweets and other presents and then ask them to accompany them to church.

7. Muslim teachers, incidentally explaining Qur'ānic verses concerning Jesus, are detained by Christian officials or calumniated. Christian youth handle such people roughly. In North Lampung, Christian authorities were successful in getting Muslim religious teachers replaced by Christian teachers. Even in the capital, in missionary schools, we find that Muslim students are not allowed to offer even Friday prayers. They are obliged to go to church.

8. Houses of Muslim families, especially in the morning when the head of the family is out and during Ramadan, are visited by missionaries with a view to influencing younger people or women. I have witnessed such visits more than ten times in my own locality.

9. Transmigration areas such as Lampung (South Sumatra), Pasaman (West Sumatra), Kendari (North Sulaweri), Mid-Sulaweri and South Borneo are

main targets of the missionary invasion. Most of the transmigrants are poor and ignorant people. The mission builds hospitals and schools for them. When the transmigrants begin to use the hospitals and schools, they are asked to build roads. When the roads are open and ready to be used, they are asked to build a church. Since there is no freedom of the press, Christian officials in the Department of Transmigration abuse their position and act as instruments of mission. Central Kalimah, which is an area far from the Central Government, is virtually governed by a Catholic Mission. Even United Nations aid, in the form of foodstuffs and other commodities, is distributed to the transmigrants through the church. To get this aid, they have to go to the church. Distribution of water pumps, seeds of cloves and coconut, etc. is also being used to serve the same purpose.

10. Undeveloped and unexplored parts of the country also enjoy high priority in covert Christianization. The islands of Mentawai, Nias, and Sumbawa are special targets. The method used by mission is that they shower gifts and provide certain facilities to isolated tribes. Then they put up a show of a census and ask these people to get themselves registered as Christians. These areas are immediately declared Christian areas. Younger people are sent to Christian schools. Modern communications are introduced to penetrate these lands. Power boats and aeroplanes are used on a vast scale. In West Kalimantan (Borneo), Christian missions have built and are operating 45 airports for landing planes and helicopters. The Government itself has only 6 such airports.

The mission has also an armada of aeroplanes in Small Sunda Island (South East Indonesia) and in West Irian. From time to time we read advertisements for employment of personnel for mission aviation.

11. Mission is active in areas known as purely Islamic, such as Aceh in North Sumatra and Banten in West Java where even the Dutch Government did not allow missionaries to work. In West Java, from Jakarta to Cigayung, Cianjur, Sukabumi and along the highway to Bandung, in the eastern part of West Java, from Kuningam southwards to Tasik Malaya, Sumedang and Garut. Along the big road between Bandung and Tasik Malaya are found many centres of mission. Majalengka which was a centre of Islamic religious education now has a seminary.

Missions have headquarters in Malang, Batu and Lawang. From these headquarters, they work at Mojokerto, Pasuruan, Jember and other places in East Java. There are mission headquarters in Kendari and Central Sulawesi (Celebes). From those places they concentrate their activities on South Sulaweri and Gorontalo, two territories famous for their Islamic spirit.

12. The latest form of this covert Christianization is in the name of modernization. Foreign missions come with money and technology. "Modernization and participation in reconstructing the country" is the new slogan. They are ready to make roads in outer islands, provide water for drinking, build

projects of irrigation, etc. But all this is not for development as such, but are steps towards Christianization. The part that education and medicine have played in the strategy of Christianization in the past is now being supplanted by a new weapon in the arsenal — the development effort.

13. In August 1973, the Indonesian Government wanted to impose a secular marriage law, disregarding religious considerations. That law was prepared by Christian experts working in a special department of the Government. When the Muslims rejected the proposed law, both Protestant and Catholic councils of churches supported the law. In other words, the Christians in Indonesia did not want Muslims to respect their own religion and follow their religious family law. All has happened, even while we remember the documents of Vatican II (p. 686), which say: "Society has the right to defend itself against possible abuses committed on pretext of freedom of religion. It is the special duty of Government to provide this protection".

Before I conclude this section, let me present very briefly the outlines of the strategy of Christianization as it emerges from a more detailed case study made by a group of Muslim workers under the guidance of Dr Muhammad Natsir.[2] This is a Study of Pasaman, a territory in West Sumatra, with a 100% Muslim population (area 764,000 ha., population 285,000 persons, of whom 220,000 are original settlers, 45,000 neighbouring tribes and 20,000 trans-migrants). The area was one of those selected for transmigration and this was used by the missions to transplant Christianity into the area. The Tapanuli tribe was among those rehabilitated in the area, and they entered as Muslims. Later it was found that some of them were Christians who posed as Muslims to gain access to the area. Similar tactics were used by some of the Javanese (Koto-Baru and Kinali) tribes.

Originally the transmigrants were welcomed by Minang Muslims in brotherly Islamic spirit. Land was given to them as Muslims. Then the Christian presence was made clear, causing much discomfort among the Muslims. Gradually more aggressive policies were pursued. For example, in Panti Rao, a Muslim gave a small piece of land to a Christian on condition that it would be used for a house and not for a church. But after the land was taken into possession, it was announced that there would be a church on that piece of land. This became known on 5th August, 1957.

On 17th August, 1957, a Christian official of the Ministry of Religious Affairs, accompanied by two ministers of the Batak Church visited the place and intended to hold services the next day. People lost patience and there was trouble.

On 29th August, 1957, a request was made to the authorities in the name of the Christian community to build a church. On 16th October, 1957, the authority

---

[2] See *Kristenisesi & Transmigresi di Sumatera Barat* (Dewan Da'wah Islamiyah Indonesia, 1975).

(Bupati Marah Amir) declined the request, saying that the Government cannot permit the building of a chuch, both because of the promise made by the newcomers from Tapanuli and also for the sake of security.

Then pressures were brought to bear by Christians from other areas, insisting in the name of freedom of religion that they should be given the right to build a church. In October 1962, the Government, after having consulted the governor, the local house of representatives, and the chief of the department of religion of the province sent a letter to the Christians, reaffirming the former decision, and saying that the Christians should not violate their understanding with the Muslims by opening a church since it would make the situation chaotic.

In spite of all that, immigrants from Tapanuli increased their number and insisted on opening a church on that land. Now Panti has a number of churches (Batak, Catholic, Adventist, Pentecostal, Bethel) while Muslims are becoming a minority in an area where after independence 100% of the population was Muslim.

In 1973, along the beach of the river Sampiur, at Panti, there arose a village called the Christian Village (Kampung Masehi). The story is almost the same as that of the Panti church. The land was given to transmigrants of Tapanuli, but in 1973 there were already 50 houses owned by smuggled Christians. It is they who gave to the village its Christian name. They sent a petition to build a church in their village. When the local authority refused, they ignored the refusal and built a church.

These are just two instances at micro-level. Now a word about the overall situation in Pasaman area. It was decided in 1953 that Pasaman should be a territory to accommodate transmigrants from Java. In the beginning everyone claimed to be Muslim and so a Muslim religious teacher was appointed by the Government. Relations between the original inhabitants and the newcomers were good. But later, it became clear that some of the transmigrants were Christians. In 1957, Catholic Javanese asked permission to build a church. The demand was refused by the Government. The situation remained calm until 1962.

In 1963, it became clear that, under instructions from the mission, Christian transmigrants to Pasaman kept their Christianity secret. Only when they were settled did they start to act collectively as Christians, demanding "freedom of religion". Formerly all transmigrants were considered guests by the original inhabitants. But the longer they stayed in their new homeland, the more their behaviour changed. As Christians occupy important Government positions in this area, they use their official position to strengthen this process of Christianization of the area.

In 1967, the Diocese of Padang made an exaggerated report to the Government, stating that the area was infested with malaria and other diseases, that education was neglected, that transmigrants were very poor and that the situation demanded immediate action.

It was at this time that the Assistant Bishop of Padang asked permission to build a permanent building for the elementary school, to open a clinic and to build a church. Almost at the same time the Bishop asked that a rice-huller be sent to a certain immigrant to help the economy of the territory.

The people of Pasaman protested against the demand of the Bishop through their organizations and their elders. The Government explained to the Bishop that it could not ignore these protests of the people of the area and give him permission to build a school, a clinic and a church and import a rice-huller. In spite of that, in 1968, the Catholics were bold enough to build a presbytery, a school and a church with a big cross. The local housing representative discussed the Catholic attitude and issued a statement saying that the Catholics had no right to build the school, the church and the clinic.

The tense situation continued for two years. The local authority underlined the problem and asked the Bishop to respect its decision. But the Bishop answered in clear and definite language that he did not recognize the decision of the Government. He even sent a protest to the President, saying that the mission was carrying out its duty in accordance with the Pancasila.

When the Government of General Suharto made the first Five Year Plan (1969-1974), the Catholics and the Diocese of Padang made a similar plan, the main sectors being education, health, welfare, church building at Panti and Kinali, communication and agriculture. Although the people of Psaaman and the local Government of Pasaman did not agree, and were supported by the local parliament and organizations in their protest, yet the Catholic and the Bishop carried out their Five Year Plan. They built a school, a clinic, and got a rice-huller without permission. The priests visited the houses of the inhabitants, gave them help in the form of rice, cloth, etc. All these activities were co-ordinated by the Bishop of Padang, and in Pasaman the business is administered by the Catholic Council of Koto Baru. This is how Christianity comes like a steamroller in Indonesia today. We find in the society of Pasaman a feeling of hatred towards Christianity. First, they regretted having given up their lands to the transmigrants; secondly, they feel frustrated because as Muslims from Muslim descendents, they feel unable to defend themselves against the Christian agression; and thirdly, they feel much depressed about giving up their religious traditions under the force of pressure from everywhere.

Secularism or Religion

The facts I have presented are distasteful. It is agonizing for us to witness these developments; it is painful to narrate them. I have done so only because I believe that we are on the edge of a volcano. If things are allowed to continue I see nothing but catastrophe. The relations between the two great religious communities of the world, the Christians and the Muslims, are bound to be affected adversely by this "religious" aggression, and it is my considered opinion that in the last round this will only pave the way for the anti-God and secularist forces to cast their spell over a people who are still attached to a universal religious tradition. If this happens, then let me say frankly, it would not be just the Muslims, but also the Christians who would suffer. There would be no victors nor losers amongst us; Muslims and Christians alike might turn out to be losers and our common enemies gain at our cost.

The situation in South East Asia has changed with the fall of South Vietnam. Thailand and Malaysia now face the communist threat. We do not know the future, but I am certain that Christianization as it is practised now in Indonesia may bring with it a new upsurge of the communist danger. Particularly with the mass conversion of the communists to Christianity after the fall of Sukarno, the communists have been given a new lease on life in the sheltering care of Christianity.

This brings me once again to one of the central issues in Indonesia. Christian missions are prepared to be in alliance with anyone, but are not prepared to see Muslims develop their individual as well as corporate life in accordance with Islam. Any effort to strengthen Islam amongst the Muslims, any effort to see that Islamic law and traditions are established in an overwhelmingly Muslim country are regarded as a threat by the Christians. Classic instances in this respect are provided by the Christian attitude to the Muslims' desire to reconstruct their socio-political life in accordance with the *sharī'ah*. Indonesia is a Muslim country. Ninety-five per cent of its population is Muslim. Our independence movement was inspired by our religion. When we attained independence in August 1945, it was agreed that the declaration would contain a statement to the effect that the Muslims would be enabled to follow the *sharī'ah*. But when the declaration was read by Dr Hatta, the Vice President-elect, this phrase was omitted. In 1975, Dr Hatta has made it known to the world that he had to omit it at the insistence of the Dutch Government who declared that it would not be acceptable to the Christians. Although a Ministry of Religious Affairs was established on that occasion, the question of declaring Islam as the basis of the State was postponed. In 1958, President Sukarno issued a presidential decree that the statement omitted in the August 1945 declaration (the injunction that Muslims could follow the *sharī'ah*) was the spirit behind the constitution. The ideology of the State, however, remained the Pancasila. The Christians have opposed every effort by the Muslims to make the *sharī'ah* the basis of Muslim corporate life in Indonesia. They have fought tooth and nail to perpetrate a secular order in the country. They have gone to the extent of opposing the Islamic Personal Statutes which are meant to enable the family law of Islam to be enforced for Muslims. Let me quote the official position of the Christians as stated in the letter of the Catholic Fraction of the House of Representatives (No. 15/FK/69, dated 1st February, 1969, with Annex 1).

"Since the Personal Statutes say that the national law follows the religious law, as explained in Article 37, we, the Catholics, feel that the Personal Statutes have

77

left the principal norms in our law, i.e. Pancasila. With the inclusion of the Personal Statutes in the Parliament, we now have two highest sources of law, i.e. preamble of the Constitution of 1945 and God's revelation."

Annex I to the letter elaborates on the theme and it deserves to be read carefully.

1.4 The difference of opinion is as follows: One party said that regulation of marriage according to the Statutes is normal and therefore acceptable. The other party said: Such regulation violates the reality of the State of Pancasila. This has a very important consequence, that is, that in every field of life, this procedure might be used. This means that the principle of our State has changed. It is no more a Pancasila State, but a religious state, in accordance with the Jakarta Charter. (Reference is to the phrase omitted at the proclamation, viz. the injunction for the Muslims to follow the *shari'ah*.)

2.1c With the possibility of regulating marriage according to religious law in the form of the Personal Statutes, we shall have more than one highest source of law — national law having its source in the Preamble of the Constitution of 1945 and religious law having revelation as its highest source.

2.1d The religious law which is promulgated as national law now should be subject to the Preamble of the Constitution of the year 1945 as the highest source of national law. But this is not possible because it will hurt the feelings of religious people. On the contrary, if we make God's revelation the highest source of national law and therefore the national law is subject to the religious law, as indicated in the Personal Statutes, then the Republic of Indonesia which we proclaimed is no more.

2.2b Therefore, the sila of belief in One God must not be understood as belonging only to the religions, as explained by the Minister of Religious Affairs in his speech as representative of the Government answering the Parliament.

2.2c Belief in one God is not the monopoly of the religions, because the Pancasila, including belief in one God, existed already in Indonesia before the arrival of the religions. It is clear therefore [according to the Catholics] that religion is not given the monopoly to exercise the sila of belief in one God.[3]

2.3 Third idea: transgression against human rights.

2.3a Religion has, as its source, personal conviction. Therefore, realization of *shari'ah* must not be forced through law.[4]

2.3b To put *shari'ah* in a law with certain sanctions against those who violate it is in reality coercion and therefore a contradiction of human rights and of Article 29 of the Constitution (which says: Every citizen has the right to embrace a religion and to observe its rituals).

2.3c Therefore, whatever we say about freedom of religion, it will mean nothing as long as there is coercion in carrying out *shari'ah*.

---

3 "The religions" here refers to Islam and Christianity and does not include various forms of animism. (IRM Eds.)
4 All this is simply baffling to a Muslim. The Islamic Personal Statute related to the Muslims and were not being imposed on non-Muslims. But the Christians object that *shari'ah* should not be introduced among the Muslims. Living in obedience to Islamic religion means accepting the sovereignty of the *shari'ah* in our lives and affairs. To drag human rights and freedom of religion into this debate is disgusting. Does not freedom of religion mean that the Muslim, who makes up 95 percent of the population, should be enabled to live according to the *shari'ah* in which they believe? Should the less than 5 percent Christians have the right to force the Muslims not to order their family life according to the Islamic law, which is their belief and conviction?

2.4a The Parliament received also a draft of judicial structure in which beside the Supreme Court there would be a *Shari'ah* Supreme Court. Here we feel that efforts to subjugate national law to religious law become clearly evident. With the establishment of a religious supreme court which will issue decisions on religious cases on the basis of God's revelations, there will be no other authority to abrogate its decision except God himself.

2.4b If we remember that God's revelation will be made the highest source of national law, and if we have in mind that religious law (in Islam) regulates all fields of life, and if we remember that we shall have a Supreme Religious Court, then we may expect that all aspects of social and political life will be subjected to that Supreme Religious Court.

2.4c From the point of view of national law, as a consequence of making God's revelation the highest source of law, we shall have many religious laws in every field of social and political life. We can imagine how complicated it will be.

I have quoted extensively from this document to show what the Christian minority is trying to impose upon the Muslim majority. In 1973, we witnessed a similar crusade. Introduction of Muslim family law for the Muslims was unanimously opposed by the Council of Churches in Indonesia (Protestant) and the High Council of Catholic Churches. In a joint statement issued on 12th December, 1973, they said:

"1. According to the Constitution of 1945, Article 29, the State guaranteed to the citizen the freedom to embrace his religion and to perform rituals according to that religion or belief. This means that the most essential thing in religion is the freedom of choice.

2. During the discussion on Personal Statutes in the Parliament, we felt an anxiety that the State would not guarantee the freedom of religion; moreover we get the impression that the State will impose religious law, at least concerning marriage.

3. We hope that every citizen will go through a marriage ceremony according to his religion, but voluntarily. But if we consider the religious marriage the only legal one, then many problems concerning religious freedom will arise."

An acrimonious debate followed in the Christian press and every pressure was used to stop the introduction of Muslim family law for the Muslims.[5] The crux of the matter was that religion must not be allowed to play a decisive role in the socio-political life of the people. The Catholic daily "Komdas" put it clearly in its editorial dated 17th December, 1973: "The application of religious law in marriage will open the possibility of further application of religious law in many other fields." This had echoes in the entire Christian press. Now this debate has once again brought into sharp focus the question that intrigues us as Muslims: if the Muslims want their socio-political system and their corporate life to be organized in accordance with their religious law, why is it unacceptable to the Christians? Christians use every artifice to see that secular law prevails, which for the Muslims virtually means de-Islamization of their collective life. If this is modernization, then we as Muslims look

---

[5] See my book: *Kasus R. U. U. Derkawinan dalam Rubuangan Islam dau Kristen* (Peneebit, Jakarta, 1974).

upon it as a form of neo-colonialism. The West has failed to see us in our true light. This tragedy has been succinctly summed up by Professor Wilfred Smith when he says:

"The Orient until now has been approached by the West chiefly on two levels — a religious level, on which the official Christian view has been that the beliefs and values of the Orient are wrong; and a secular level, in which the official view has been, and remains today, that their belief and values do not matter.

"The fact is that to the men concerned these beliefs and values matter a very great deal. They matter not only in the sense that their adherent cherishes them, regarding them as supremely precious. More subtly and elementally, he thinks by means of them, feels in term of them and acts by them, and for them, and through them even when he is thinking, feeling and acting in the matter that we regard as political and economic." [6]

To us, Islam determines our identity, individual as well as social. If Christianity is trying to force secularism on the world of Islam, then we are in boats moving in opposite directions.

In this paper I have tried to present the feelings of the Muslim world as I honestly feel and share them. I hope the Christian world will try to peep into our hearts. We want co-operation between the worlds of Islam and Christianity but healthy co-operation can take place only if we are prepared to be just and honest to each other and above all be honest to God Whom we want to serve and not the thousand and one gods that have taken hold of the human race. I hope and pray we still can evolve a framework for living together in peace and justice and to bring an end to exploitation of the weak by the powerful, of the poor by the rich, of the underdeveloped by the developed, of the common man by the clever elite that is so rampant — and worst of all rampant even in the name of religion.

A MUSLIM EXPERIENCE OF CHRISTIAN MISSION IN EAST AFRICA

ALI MUHSIN BARWANI

Former Deputy Prime Minister and Minister for External Affairs, Zanzibar

The story of Christian-Muslim relations in East Africa at the time of and after the advent of Islam was one of tolerance, mutual respect and healthy cooperation. Scriptural evidence, both canonical and apocryphal, exists which could have given the Christians of Arabia and its environs hope of the coming of a Prophet who would vindicate the basis of their faith in God and Jesus Christ. It was in that atmosphere that the Prophet Muhammad (peace be upon him) in the fifth year of his mission sent out a group of his followers

---

6 Wilfred C. Smith: *The Faith of Other Men* (New York: Harper and Row, 1963) pp. 104-5.

to Ethiopia to escape the persecution of his idolatrous kinsmen. Ethiopia was a Christian country. That the refugees were well received is recorded history. When they appeared before the King to answer the charges of the envoys of the idolatrous Quraish who demanded their extradition, the spokesman of the refugees, Ja'far bin Abi Talib, the Prophet's cousin answered in these memorable words:

> We were folk immersed in ignorance, worshipping idols, eating carrion, given to lewdness, severing the ties of kinship, bad neighbours, the strong among us preying upon the weak; thus were we till Allah sent to us a messenger of our own, whose lineage, honesty, trustworthiness and chastity we knew, and he called us to Allah that we should acknowledge His unity and worship Him and eschew all the stones and idols that we and our fathers used to worship beside Him; and ordered us to be truthful and to restore the pledge and observe the ties of kinship, and be good neighbours, and to abstain from things forbidden, and from blood, and forbade us lewdness and false speech, and to prey upon the wealth of orphans and to accuse good women; and commanded us to worship Allah only, ascribing no one unto Him as partner and enjoined us prayer and legal alms and fasting. ... And when they [the Mekkans] persecuted and oppressed us, and hemmed us in, and kept us from the practice of our religion, we came forth to thy land, and chose thee above all others, and sought thy protection, and hoped that we should not be troubled in thy land, O King![1]

Thus did Islam enter Africa. Several years before the teachings of the Prophet were received in Madinah they had reached East Africa. Among the Prophet's earliest and staunchest followers were men and women of East African origin. Baraka or Umm Aymana embraced Islam with Ali the very next day of the Prophet's revelation. She was an East African, and she had been the one who had looked after the Prophet when as a child he lost his mother. Bilal, the Prophet's muezzin, who bore all that human endurance should bear, was also of East African descent. Similarly was Sumayya who became the first person to lay down her life for her faith.

Not an alien faith in East Africa, Islam came overland in the first decade with the refugees to Ethiopia, and by sea in the first century with the seamen who were always visiting the East African coast. There are, however, no indications that Christianity penetrated south of Ethiopia and Sudan until the coming of the Portuguese by sea round the Cape. Both religions, Islam and Christianity, are missionary religions. The East Africans, however, have seen that their approaches and methods differ fundamentally. The spread of Islam has never been an organized affair in East Africa. By living his religion the Muslim imperceptibly helps to propagate his faith. He does not have to preach as a professional, although he may not lack argument when argument is called for. Lyndon Harries writes in his book *Islam in East Africa :* "Islam, like Christianity, is a missionary religion, but the missionary as we know him has a more important place in East Africa amongst Christians than amongst Muslims". And further on he expounds: "Islam depends almost entirely for

---

[1] Translated by Muhammad Marmaduke Pickthall from *Sirah Ibn Hisham*, Cairo Edition, Part 1, p. 116.

the spread of its faith upon the influence of the Muslim community. When social distinctions are overcome, the progress of conversion is likely to be accelerated."

Harries goes on to say:

> The Portuguese intended to destroy Islam, to secure the gold traffic of Sofala, to dominate the Indian Ocean and to banish all Muslims from its waters, to break the monopoly which the Islamic peoples held of the wealthy trade with India, and to divert it by way of the new Cape route into the coffers of Portugal. This was a "Christian" war, to be compared, as to its spirit, with the Crusades, but it was a dark chapter, not only in Islamic but in Christian history as well.

The Portuguese attempt at "civilizing and Christianizing" was a total failure in East Africa north of Mozambique, although they ruled it for two hundred years. They left practically nothing worthwhile in their wake except tales of woe and destruction and, on the entrance of Mombasa harbour, that monstrous pile of forbidding rock ironically called Fort Jesus. Times change and conditions differ, but aims persist. The Portuguese are driven out. The Islamic way of life regains its freedom. Swahili literature gets new impetus with the liberation. Mosques and mansions are rebuilt, and plantations of cloves, coconuts and orchards containing every tropical and subtropical fruit are laid out. Inter-city and international trade comes to life again. But that is not to last long. The crude Portuguese way was a failure. Now things must be done more scientifically, more humanely.

David Livingstone, the 19th century version of Vasco da Gama, came as an explorer and a missionary. His motives are clear in the statement made at the University of Cambridge on 4th December, 1857 and quoted by Stephen Neill in his book *A History of Christian Missions:* "I go back to Africa to try to make an open path for commerce and Christianity". When Livingstone discovered Shire Highlands in 1860 he wrote: "I am becoming every day more sure that English colonization is necessary to our real success. In this new area of Highlands the greatest good could be done by developing trade in cotton and checking trade in slaves." In another context Livingstone said: "Sending the Gospel to the pagans must include more than is suggested by the usual picture of a missionary namely a man going about with a Bible under his arm. The development of commerce ought especially to be attended to." (T. R. Batten, *Tropical Africa in World History*)

David Livingstone was not perhaps a colonialist by nature. His primary motive was legitimate commerce, and he saw that the end could not be achieved without using the means of outright colonization to bring peace and stability. It was therefore a question of the means justifying the end in the same way as the abolition of the slave trade; for how could slaves acquire the purchasing power to buy Manchester goods? This might sound cynical and an attempt at imputing motives without justification, but this is what critics have said.

If the abolition of the slave trade had sprung purely from humanitarian motivation, then colonization should not have been its necessary corollary. Indeed if it had been, then the Portuguese territories of Angola and Mozambique should have long been expropriated from those who conducted a more vicious trade in human beings than ever existed in East Africa. Similarly it would have been the possessions of Western powers in West Africa from which 800% more slaves were being exported annually and with much greater cruelty than from East Africa. In any case, merely to alter the type of slavery is not something to write home about.

Ironically enough, it is this that the Christian missions in East Africa talk most about, and it is with the stick of slavery that they try to beat the Muslims the hardest. The general tendency with the missionary was not to stick to the truth. Facts were there to be coloured, magnified, and even bent and distorted for a purpose, if the purpose was considered noble and holy enough. The Arabs practised slavery. It was evil, and it must be condemned in the strongest terms. But it was an evil that was shared by all; indeed, if the truth were known, it would seem that they were not among the worst offenders. But it suited public relations for the missionary in East Africa to paint the Arabs in the most repulsive colours, and, not merely by implication, to attribute what some Arabs did as being an evil implicit in Islam. Sir Arthur Hardinge, British Consul General in Zanzibar, nauseated by the distortions of the missionary reports on the question of the abolition of slavery in Zanzibar, wrote to Lord Salisbury that they made him realize why apparently otherwise humane Roman Emperors "so cruelly persecuted the early Christians". The commander of HMS *Phoebe*, Captain MacGill had also a very low opinion of certain missionaries in Pemba. He regarded them as unfitted either to form or to express an opinion on the question of the freeing of slaves in a Muslim country. He wrote that it was a pity that they were not forced to retire "into the obscurity for which they are so eminently fitted". (L. W. Hollingsworth: *Zanzibar Under the Foreign Office*.)

Bishop Fogarty of Damaraland, speaking of the progress being made in South Africa, said: "The universal brotherhood established by Islam only, in the world, is a potent factor for bringing slavery to an end, though war-captivity will, on the other hand, continue as long as war exists in the world. But I would ask my Arab co-religionists to reflect that if they purchase slaves from these negro lands they are acting against the teachings of their own Prophet." Canon Broomfield of the UMCA Zanzibar. His book, *Colour Conflict in Africa* is worth reading. But how rare are such birds!

The long memory of the illiterate African has been dulled by the introduction of the written word whose magic has literally charmed him into believing whatever he is given to read by his mentor. The school textbooks, the press, secular and religious, the radio and the pulpit, all of these have been geared to present the turbanned Muslim as a cruel, polygamous, bloodthirsty, reactionary slave driver whose existence cumbers the earth. The disorganized Muslims who welcomed the first missionaries and gave them every assistance in carrying out their task were appalled at the way things turned out. The missionaries, instead of concentrating on all the good they could speak of about their own faith, spent a good deal of time and effort denigrating the Islamic faith. Statements like that of the former Archbishop of East Africa, Beecher, that Islam was a greater danger to Africa than international communism and African nationalism could not be conducive to harmonious relations between the adherents of the two faiths.

Many waves have tried to engulf the Muslims in East Africa. The Crusades, the two hundred years of Portuguese occupation, the First World War and its aftermath which abolished the Caliphate, the colonial period — all these delivered heavy blows to Islam. During the Colonial period four African Muslim leaders — two Kikuyu, one Mkamba and one Luo in Kenya sent a memorandum to the Joint Select Committee on Closer Union in East Africa in 1931. "The memorandum expressed the fear that trends in the country worked against Islam, which was thus threatened with extinction, just as it had been broken in Uganda prior to that territory being taken over by the British. The African Muslim leaders complained that while 'fabulous sums of money' were being expended on Christian missionary societies from funds to which Muslims of all races contributed, the government in all three territories of East Africa 'remains a silent witness to the gradual process of discouragement of Islam and its death by a deliberate policy of denying to it any opportunity of surviving, while every possible encouragement and preference is being given directly to Christianity to sweep the whole of Eastern Africa."[2]

Islam is the religion of a majority of the people of East Africa. But the Muslims are faced with a new form of slavery — arbitrary rule and political suffocation. And their new rulers are not colonialists from abroad but people belonging to the Christian minority group, people who are the products of the colonial era of the missions and who still enjoy their blessings. I wonder why one form of slavery was bad and why this new form of slavery is not considered obnoxious.

□▣□

Preliminary to general discussion of the papers on Indonesia and East Africa, Mr Ali Muhsin made a few further comments: (Editors)

Ali Muhsin: I would like to draw attention to the Muslim experience of education in East Africa which, during the colonial period, was entirely in the hands of Christian missionaries — as were the hospitals. Education is a principal means of moulding people's minds, and the colonial governments left this in the hands of Christian missions of various denominations. This had the effect of alienating the Muslims: either Muslim parents kept their children away from school for fear that education at the hands of a Christian would lead inevitably to their conversion to Christianity, or they let their children go to school without caring whether or not they would be converted.

---

[2] A. I. Salim: *The Swahili-Speaking Peoples of Kenya's Coast*, East African Publishing House, pp. 165-166.

The overall result was that the Muslims remained on the whole backward educationally, and they developed no education system of their own apart from the traditional Qur'ān schools where they were taught little more than reading and writing the Qur'ān, and how to say their prayers. The majority of Muslims remained in ignorance, so that when modern administration came, it fell largely into the hands of the Christians, and this remains so today even though the Christians are a minority in the East African countries.

Ahmad: I must certainly say that we Muslims do feel that Christian missionary education — and here I echo Mr Ali Muhsin — has been partly responsible for leading the Muslim educated elite away from their religious traditions, with the result that the new leadership which has emerged in the Muslim world during and after the colonial period lacks moral and religious commitment. Christian missions in the Muslim world have failed to convert Muslims to Christianity, but they have succeeded in driving quite an important number of Muslims away from Islam towards secularism. The net result has been the loss of religious commitment and a decline in moral values and of a moral approach to life.

Sanneh: It is not true to give the impression that Christians have put all their eggs in the secular basket, and that they have abandoned their spiritual and religious responsibilities in favour of the secularism which surrounds them. Christians are united with Muslims in their concern to live under God, to obey him, and to check the anti-religious forces in society.

Ali Muhsin: Another factor in the East African experience is that some of the Christian missionaries have allowed themselves to become advocates of the political cause of Zionism, and some of their literature provides clear evidence for this. In my view the most imperialistic radio station in the world is the Voice of the Gospel. It has a long history of pro-Zionism and has only moderated its views in light of recent political events in Africa.

Sanneh: My own experience has been that it is amongst the Christian missionaries most deeply involved in the life of Muslim countries, in the Middle East and elsewhere, that we find some of the most loyal friends of the Arabs in the West. Many missionaries have played a leading role in the distribution of Palestinian literature in the West. They have written their own often very controversial biblical critiques of Zionism and the state of Israel, and they have lobbied western governments with letters of protest about western policy towards Israel. So there are many Christians deeply devoted to the Bible who as deeply resent the misuse of the Bible for political purposes.

I want to make a plea therefore that we recognize not only negative but also the positive aspects of missionary activity, and that in due respect of the latter we look for areas of co-operation between Christians and Muslims in our response to the call of God. We need to build confidence in each other for each other.

Mr Irfan widened the discussion to include the situation in Indonesia: (Editors)

Irfan: Our basic business, it seems to me, is not the ventilation of certain grievances or the hurling of accusations, or opening certain old wounds. Our basic aim here is to try to share with those whom one regards as friends a very important and practical aspect of Muslim-Christian relationship. This sharing of experience is an obvious necessity. Surely it is pleasant to no one to talk of differences, yet there is no other way to resolve them than to face them.

In this light, the situation, according to Dr Rasjidi and Mr Muhsin in Indonesia and Tanzania is deserving of examination by all those who take a moral and spiritual view of their vocation. Both Indonesia and Tanzania are Muslim majority countries, but in the nature of things, Muslims do not appear to enjoy effective freedom and sovereignty over their own affairs. On the other hand they have the feeling of being pushed into a situation of helplessness and discriminated against. If we all agree proselytization is wrong and immoral then the details given by Dr Rasjidi about underhanded and unfair missionary practices in Indonesia should present no problem of judgement or opinion to a religious conscience.

However, what I regard as more central to the whole problem is the basic Christian attitude toward the Muslim's aspiration to live in a corporate Islamic society in accordance with his understanding of the divine guidance. I think Muslim-Christian relations will improve tremendously if this question could be answered positively. Personally, I do appreciate the Christian desire to "save" the Muslim soul in accordance with their understanding of the Divine Truth, but the question we face is whether the Muslim has a right to an Islamic society until it is possible to convince him otherwise.

Unfortunately, there is no unequivocal answer to this question and in the absence of such an answer, one is led to suspect that perhaps some people see the path of conversion beginning in the subversion of Muslim values and social fibre. Dr Rasjidi did cite the example of why *"sharī'ah* law for Muslims" could not be incorporated into Indonesia's constitution because of a foreign-backed Christian veto. Things went even further when churches in Indonesia began to advocate and support the imposition of secular family law on Indonesian Muslims. In my view this is a very, very serious matter because there is evidence of similar efforts in other countries and other situations, where one finds Christians, to his pain and surprise, to be more in sympathy with the situation where a Muslim can become secular or even communist rather than remaining a practising Muslim. The de-Islamization of Muslims may no doubt appear to be tempting as a step towards his eventual "Christianization", but would that also be true Christian witness? This makes the vast range of Christian mission in the Muslim world acquire a negative image. The church is seen not as inviting people to the teachings of Jesus (peace and blessings of God be upon him), but trying to subvert or seduce Muslims from practising Islam.

The church in Indonesia may not be in league with old imperial powers, but there is no doubt that it is being wholly and on a very vast scale financed by funds which come from the former colonial countries. Under the circumstances suspicion about neo-colonial links are therefore only natural. These, the recently discovered CIA links with Christian missionaries and my own knowledge about some high-ranking churchmen being involved — among others — in the tragic politics leading to the bifurcation of the biggest Muslim state of Pakistan, make it appropriate to draw the attention of our Christian friends to a situation where the line between mission proper and covert politics seems to have become blurred.

I think we ought to welcome this discussion of grievances in so far as this can be useful in removing the negatives in Muslim-Christian relations and improving the state and quality of their dialogue. Without enlarging the scope of our discussions, I could go a step further and suggest a re-evaluation, by our Christian friends, of the whole range of overseas missions from a strictly Christian point of view. In this respect, the African continent — wherein the vast majority of governmental leadership and national elites are either Christian or the product of Christian educational institutions — would provide an ideal case study.

I think, given the right spirit, the problem is not impossible of solution. Don't we agree that *diakonia* is not mission proper and if used as a vehicle for influence or propaganda, it becomes ulterior and unchristian? There already is a suggestion put forward by some churches to place a moratorium on overseas mission. And there has been talk here of a code of conduct. Perhaps some or all of these could be considered in this context, but the most important thing first of all is a moral recognition of the problem.

Ihromi: All of us in Indonesia feel a terrible frustration arising out of a deep sense of alienation on the part of both Christians and Muslims. The Christian in Indonesia is always identified as a puppet of outside powers, rather than as a citizen of Indonesia. But what we Christians of Indonesia yearn for is to be regarded as Indonesian just as we regard our Muslim brothers as Indonesian. The ideal of a single citizenship — common citizens, "concitoyens" — is what we must strive for in Indonesia — equal rights for everybody as common citizens of a single state.

al-Faruqi: Professor Ihromi seems to be yearning for a state in Indonesia in very much the same terms as the western state — a centralized state in which all citizens obey the same laws. It is a real pity that Asians and Africans should yearn after the kind of state which was born out of intellectual and spiritual movements in Europe beginning with the Reformation and finishing in nineteenth century Romanticism. It is these movements which have brought about the notion of the state as a single monolithic body. In Islam we have a different concept of the state — a state truly as a servant of the people rather than their master, a state ruling to preserve public order, but still giving freedom to the various minorities within the state to exist, survive and prosper.

87

The idea of every "citoyen" — the very term is charged with European Romanticism — being a duplicate of every other "citoyen", is foreign to the spirit and traditions of Islam. But the western mind is incapable of conceiving of a state which is not monolithic in nature.

Taylor: While taking the Muslim grievances which we have heard about very seriously, we have had a tremendous emphasis in our discussion on mission as it was practised in the nineteenth century, and perhaps amongst certain fringe groups today. If we want to talk about what is actually happening today, then we must take much more seriously the criticisms which have been made of the abuse of mission by the churches in Africa and Asia and by many Christians in the West. And Muslims would find a rather favourable response amongst many Christian missionaries themselves.

Ahmad: Permit me to say that there is some kind of an understanding gap, and not merely a communication gap, between Christians and Muslims on this point. When a critique of colonialism is made, people in the West say they agree, but insist that colonialism is now dead. When criticisms are made of missions, people say this was true of the eighteenth and nineteenth centuries, but no longer today. I may not necessarily be right, but if I understand the Muslim mind correctly, I must say that the Muslims feel that the names have changed but that the substance has not. We are still dealing with the same realities in different garb. In the field of colonialism we have come to the much more dangerous area of concealed colonialism, neo-colonialism. Now it is very possible that our Muslim reaction is subjective, but you must realize that this is our reaction, and that it is a real and honest reaction. Even in the area of mission, the facts of exploitation and mission we are referring to relate to 1960s and '70s and not to an earlier age.

al-Faruqi: It is much more honest to say that we realize that neo-colonialism is a force, and that here in this consultation we are trying to discover ways and means of saying what, within our spheres of power, we will do about it. I personally do not agree to discuss with anyone who argues that there is no neo-colonialism today in, for example, Indonesia. And what concerns us very much here is the linkage between the missionary movement and neo-colonialism. If you don't see that Christians in places like Tanzania and Indonesia are being used by imperialist forces, then there is no point in our continuing our conversation.

Ihromi: But we Christians in Indonesia feel a deep sense of solidarity with our Muslim fellow-citizens. We would like to see the growth of a sense of single citizenship shared by Muslims and Christians in Indonesia. You seem to disregard this when you accuse all the Christians in Indonesia of being in the hands of neo-colonial powers.

Hajjar: The argument seems to have become a vicious circle. But perhaps there is a way out of the impasse if we define our terms more clearly. If we speak about mission and insist upon connecting mission with colonialism, then we simply get stuck. What Muslims rightly object to is not mission itself but the proselytism of western missionaries, who come to the Muslim world to try to convert Muslims by various means to Christianity. But I think it is important that we should make this distinction between mission and proselytism, as the Catholic Church has always tried to do. Proselytism is the ugly face of mission. Now I agree that mission cannot simply be abstracted from its wider social, cultural and political context, particularly the context of European colonialism, but we must try to preserve the distinction between mission in its ideal, about which we have heard much already, and proselytism about which we have also heard. Muslims have very real grievances, but I would enlarge the word "proselytism" to include any form of European imposition on the Muslim world, not only by western missionaries but perhaps more importantly today by the mass media and the extensive literature which advocates the cause of secularism. Many of the Arab intellectuals, for example, are proselytisers in this sense, and this poses a much more serious threat to Arab Muslim societies today than the missionaries. Syria — my own country — closed its doors to all missionaries several years ago, but today it faces a terrible problem of the penetration of secularism.

DISCUSSION ON RELIGIOUS FREEDOM

An issue which came up at several points during the discussions was that of religious freedom, and we here reproduce excerpts of what was said, with particular attention to the implications for religious freedom of the Islamic concern for a religious state on the one hand, and western notions of secularism on the other. (Editors)

Rudvin: I want to go back to the point about African tolerance which Sanneh raised in his paper — the fact that in African families Christians and Muslims can live together under the same roof, without trouble. If we all could imitate and follow this I think it would be a great thing.

I find that a basic problem with mission to Muslims, and in Pakistan at least it is the same with Islamic *da'wah* to Christians, is that we don't allow a real functional religious freedom to one another. Surely one of the main reasons for the negative attitudes between Muslims and Christians is the treatment meted out to converts, probably on both sides. In Pakistan I would go so far as to say that a convert in a major city will survive with his life, but probably not so in a village. I do not mean this as a criticism. Three hundred years ago the same was true of Norway, where a convert from Christianity would have had to leave the kingdom. Now I feel very strongly that one of the ground rules for Christian mission and Islamic *da'wah* should be functional religious freedom for both sides: that we as Christian and Muslim leaders should tell those for whom we are responsible not to abuse converts, not to ostracize them from the family nor from society, making them lose their inheritance, their jobs, etc. Rather there should be a true tolerance within the family and thus within society at large.

Ahmad: I agree that religious freedom, like any other freedom, is important but it has to be within certain limits and within a certain framework. No freedom is unlimited; indeed unlimited freedom is a contradiction in terms. It is only through limitations that freedom becomes freedom, otherwise it degenerates into licence and anarchy. Thus when a religious system is concerned not merely to provide for the spiritual reform and uplift of the individual, but to go on to create the framework of the social and community life of a state — as in Islam — freedom can only have meaning within this framework and not outside it. I hope our Christian brothers can be sensitive to this, particularly since in their case, perhaps, faith has not been so strong a determining factor in the shaping and colouring of social institutions and political institutions, as has been the case in Islam. The Muslim state, and the Muslim family, derives its identity, character and authority from Islam, and tries to develop a framework of social rights and obligations on the basis of the *shari'ah*, the Islamic Law, on the basis, therefore, of divine guidance. In such a society, if a person accepts Islam as his faith, he subjects himself to that law, and his function as a Muslim then depends upon his obedience to that law. This point deserves to be kept in mind, particularly where Christians are of the view that Muslims and Christians could get on much better together within a secular state. You see, even the idea of a family giving up its religious basis in favour of a tolerance of give-and-take religiosity should be anathema to Islam, for it is part of a dangerous process of de-Islamization.

I must also state clearly that the Islamic position about freedom to leave the fold of Islam and the Muslim community is defined by the Islamic law itself. Islam does not want anyone to enter its fold in an irresponsible way. It wants him to examine everything properly and fully and embrace it only if he is fully convinced of its truth. Then Islam is not merely a religion in the limited sense of the word involving some metaphysical doctrines and some religious rites and rituals; it is a complete way of life and a code of socio-political behaviour. It establishes a community and a state on the foundations of the faith. Faith is not just like an overcoat which one may put on and put off as one likes. It is also the foundation of the state. Change of loyalty in faith has implications for loyalty to the state. Human freedom has been fully guaranteed in the Islamic framework but like every socio-political system it is set in a network of rights, obligations and limitations. Change of faith *per se* is different from change of faith involving dislocation and rearrangement of a whole network of relationships. Conversion outside the Islamic state, or along with leaving the Islamic state is treated differently from conversion within the state. Similarly conversion which has no political or social implications for the society is treated differently from one which has such implications. It would be unfair to judge an ideological state on the criteria of a *laissez faire* state cast in the image of nineteenth century liberalism.

So I would like to hear from the Christians what their attitude really is towards the Muslim yearning and effort to have an Islamic society and an Islamic state in the places in which they constitute the majority of the population and are in a position, therefore, to fashion their social and political life according to the values of Islam. If, in such a situation, the sympathies of the Christians are with secularism, which Muslims see as the denigration of Islam as a social and political force, then we are not moving towards a situation where we can really have co-operation, but rather towards a situation which will engender real antagonisms. So while we have addressed ourselves to theological matters in this conference, trying to determine our differences and to accept our differences, we must also address ourselves to social and political matters.

Rudvin: I think it is important to say that a secular state does not mean an anti-religious state, nor does it mean a state in which religion is not allowed to play a role. Religion — perhaps we should better say "religions" — are permitted to play a role but not to the exclusion of other ideologies. However, this doesn't mean that their influence is any less direct; indeed, freed of the inevitable constraints of formal alliance with the political rule of the state, they are able to make a much deeper and much more serious impact upon all aspects of the state's life, far beyond the superficial level which has usually been the case in so-called religious states. I believe also that within a secular state it would be much easier for Christianity and Islam to co-operate to a much greater extent in bringing moral influence to bear.

al-Faruqi: But a secular state would, by definition, be opposed to the moral armament of Islam or of Christianity. If a state is secular, it will not be ready to derive its inspiration from any religion whatsoever. Only in an Islamic state would the moral influence of Islam really create the sort of citizen whom we aspire to produce.

Fitzgerald: But this raises an important point. I understand from Dr al-Faruqi's paper that Islamic da'wah includes the right "to convince and be convinced". The question now in my mind is: how does this work inside the framework of the Islamic state? Under the divine guidance which you say is the basis of the Islamic state, how do you define the limits in respect of religious freedom?

How far, for example, are the non-Muslims free to practise their faith, and would this include mission? Would there be a freedom to marry whomsoever one wishes, whether one is a man or a woman? To what extent would religious authority impose limits on the exercise of individual freedom; would this deprive people of what I consider to be the legitimate right of changing religious affiliation according to conscience — to de-Christianize, to de-Judaize, even to de-Muslimize?

al-Faruqi: In an Islamic state tolerance would always be shown towards the non-Muslim; this is a fundamental principle of Islam laid down in the Qur'ān. Within the Islamic state, the Islamic *ummah* as we call it in Arabic, there is a

91

place for *ummahs* of non-Muslims who are allowed to live according to their law, with their own social and political institutions, with their own religion and their own language. They are fully accepted in the sense of being allowed to live within and alongside the Muslim *ummah*. This is known as the *millet* system, and it is what our Islamic constitution, established by the Prophet Muhammad (peace be upon him), had always insisted upon. I know of no other political constitution which enshrines a comparable principle of religious tolerance. Has any western state ever even conceived of allowing a comparable social and political sovereignty to the religious communities under its jurisdiction? Take, for example, the experience of the Jews in Europe; the only situation in which they have been able to live their lives fully as Jews has been in the ghettos. In modern western states the principle of sovereignty has demanded of the Jew that he merge himself into the body of the state and so de-Judaize himself. So the cruel option which the Jews have experienced in the West has been either to live out their Jewishness and face persecution, or to de-Judaize in order to be accepted. And it was this situation which caused western Jews to develop Zionism.

But in an Islamic state, under an Islamic constitution, the Jew, and likewise the Christian, is given the liberty to live according to the obligations of his religion with dignity, in freedom and without persecution. This system of the Islamic state represents the humanistic ideal which no other system has so far been able to match.

Cragg: But we are talking not about freedom of belief, or of religious practice, but the freedom of movement of belief; and there is a radical difference between these two. A faith which you are not free to leave becomes a prison, and no self-respecting faith should be a prison for those within it.

al-Faruqi: But this is what the Islamic law is talking about. If a person converts and leaves the Muslim community, the law recognizes that he becomes the member of another community which has its own religious laws — and the competence of these laws is acknowledged by the *shari'ah*.

Fitzgerald: But we must come back to Bishop Rudvin's earlier observation and ask again: is this *de jure* principle of freedom of religious belief and movement of belief — that is to say, conversion — really permitted in fact? If so, why is such a stigma attached to the person who converts out of Islam?

al-Faruqi: But let me remind you when you talk about stigma that we are not talking about an Islamic state acting under Islamic law, but a village group or a city group aroused by the idea that they have lost one of their members so they go and kill him or put difficulties in his path. This is not an application of the Islamic law. Islamic law *does* allow a person to exit from the Islamic state.

However, the Islamic state has, of course, to protect itself — and as was said already in an earlier session — conversion so often seems to be tantamount to subversion of Islamic values and existence.

This was the situation certainly which existed in the original Islamic state in Madinah during the prophet's life, where for a person to convert out of Islam meant joining the polytheistic camp of Makkah which was in a constant state of war against the Muslims. Now obviously that was the situation in which, for political reasons, legislation was formulated that conversion out of Islam is not to be tolerated. When, later, Islam became dominant in Madinah and Makkah, and subsequently built an empire for itself, this legislation continued to be observed although you might argue that there was empirically no use for it; conversion represented no threat at all to the security of the Muslim community.

But would you really consider revoking that legislation altogether and grant unrestricted freedom to anyone to change his religion according to the Islamic principle that everyone has the right "to convince and be convinced", when we have heard of what is happening in Indonesia? What we have heard about the situation confronting Islam in Indonesia is like a re-enactment of Madinah and Makkah. When politics gets so intermingled with Christian mission, what sort of situation would you expect if total religious freedom were allowed? Give us the assurance that political involvement in mission will cease, and that power politics will no longer intrude, then the principles of religious freedom would be approved by every sensible Muslim on earth. We Muslims are at the receiving end of the line of injustice. We haven't emerged yet from two centuries of colonialization.

Rudvin: I think, Dr al-Faruqi, you are being too pessimistic. Take the situation of Western Europe, and there is no doubt that Islam is on the move; and, as far as I see things generally, there are many more Christians becoming Muslims than the other way round. I think we can also assure you that the churches represented in the World Council would be the first to insist that political means should not be used in mission and conversion. Now I implore you to understand that for western Christians in particular, though for Christians generally also, the principle of freedom of conscience, and the freedom of religion, is so important that we cannot deny it or limit it in any way without denying both man and God.

But I have another point that I want to raise, though we have discussed it in an earlier session. Dr al-Faruqi has just spoken of the situation in Madinah and Makkah during Muhammad's life. This brings me back to the issue of *jihād*. I think we often pass too easily over the first hundred years of Islamic history which had such a great impact on Christian attitudes towards Islam. I feel it would be extremely helpful if orthodox Islam would repudiate *jihād* as an aggressive concept as the Ahmadiyyah have done. I would like to see Muslim leaders and Christian leaders state quite categorically that they repudiate the use of any sort of force for any reason whatsoever.

Ahmad: *Jihād* represents to Muslims an effort to strive seriously and ceaselessly to fulfil the divine will in human life. Now *jihād* takes many forms. The first form is the fight against one's own self in order to subdue the *nafs al-ammārah*, and subordinate it to the divine will. *Jihād* also means striving to spread the word of God, to share it with others, and here in the juridic formulations *jihād* has an important place in the relations between the Islamic state and the non-Muslim world. *Jihād* is not merely war, for it involves firstly peaceful pursuits, but war definitely has its place within the total spectrum of *jihād*.

But remember this: those of us who are familiar with international relations know that, whatever the sweet platitudes, war has an important place in any law of nations. Now wars can be defensive and just wars, or wars of aggression. The war of aggression Islam rules out because Islam has come to bring the end of aggression and establish peace. But the defensive and just war are accepted principles of international law and international relations, and Islam fully acknowledges them. It has made elaborate law in respect of both the defensive and the just war, laying down important conditions which must be fulfilled. In this sense what Islam affirms is, in principle, accepted in the United Nations Charter and there must be no scaremongering on account of *jihād*.

Now I must say that the Ahmadi position on *jihād*, which Bishop Rudvin mentioned, can in no way be considered as being expressive of the Islamic doctrine. Indeed, we feel that it is a corruption of the true Islamic position which came about very much as the result of a surrender to the European colonial powers who were anxious to undermine Muslim ideas about *jihād* which were being used to organize a just war against European imperialism — what we today call a war of liberation and which, I understand, even the World Council of Churches has supported in certain cases. So this attack on the Islamic conception of *jihād* came both from the outside and from a fifth column within. Therefore the Ahmadi contribution is not something to which we should pay tribute. To the Muslim it represents an effort by the Western imperialists to undermine one of the principles of Islam which posed a threat to their hegemony. I must also set the record straight that Muslims do not regard the Ahmadiyyah as a part of the Muslim *ummah*.

□□□□□□□□□□□□□□□□□□□□□□□□□□□□□□□□□□□□□

TOWARDS A MODUS VIVENDI

The latter part of the consultation was devoted to a consideration of more practical aspects of mission and da'wah. The participants were invited to submit to the co-chairmen lists of such issues and areas of concern as they wished to see on the agenda for immediate discussion under the title "Towards a Modus Vivendi" between Christians engaged in mission and Muslims engaged in da'wah. The co-chairmen assembled the submissions under six general points, which were then introduced from the chair by Khurshid Ahmad. (Editors)

Ahmad: We now move from general issues to more specific matters which have, we believe, an important bearing on the future. You will probably agree with me that it is too early to expect consensus even on the formulation of the issues. Nonetheless we have before us six matters, though these by no means exhaust all the points we would like to discuss; I hope we shall be able to discuss others in future meetings. But the six matters to which we have to give priority now are the following:

1. By what criteria can we distinguish legitimate mission and *da'wah* activity from illegitimate activity?
2. What are the requirements and limitations of religious freedom?
3. How do we encourage mutual respect for the legitimate activities of mission and *da'wah*?
4. By what practical methods can we make effective our repudiation of what we see to be illegitimate activities of mission and *da'wah*?
5. How can Christians and Muslims co-operate in what is an imperative of their respective faiths, that is, to serve their fellow men in need?
6. What recommendations do we wish to make regarding future studies, dialogues and other activities?

Now I hope that as our discussion proceeds we might be able to reach the point of making certain recommendations, giving a more practical orientation to our deliberations.

From our discussions so far the one fact which has emerged clearly is that the means of Christian evangelism have not been exclusively those of preaching and discussion, but that economic, educational and social inducements have been used, together with the exploitation of weaknesses — illness, political dependence, etc. This is a crucial issue, and it comes to light because of the intermingling of religion and political exploitation by some Christian missionaries in the Muslim world. We recognize also that there could be some instances of Christians feeling that Muslims have not respected Christian rights. Could we start then by identifying as one of the basic criteria in (1), that religious discussion must be divorced from any direct or indirect exploitation of people's weaknesses, or their political and social disadvantage. And that the wrongs of the past should be rectified as far as possible to pave the way for more effective co-operation in the future.

Rudvin: I think we could approach this more positively. Besides being a church administrator and organizing church work in Pakistan I am a missionary and evangelist to Muslims. For me, and for the vast majority of evangelists to Muslims what we most fear is that anybody should convert to Christianity for motives other than pure faith. This is a basic issue we should consider, as none of us wants anybody to convert if they don't really believe. So let us say that we repudiate any secondary motives in conversion: that what we are most afraid of on both sides is a person becoming a Christian or Muslim for impure motives.

Irfan: I think it would be more realistic if we asked the Christians to lay down for themselves what in their view is unethical, immoral and thus unchristian activity in mission. Similarly the Muslims could draw up such a list. That would be a great achievement, and would be more realistic since neither side would need to adhere to criteria which it does not fully accept. But it would be the beginning of a certain awareness on both sides.

Fitzgerald: Of course Christians recognize that there have been wrongs in the past and that they still continue today. The fact that we want to establish a code of missionary behaviour in consultation with the Muslims proves this. But can we not come back to Bishop Rudvin's point and say that we desire people to embrace faith, or change allegiance, because of belief — and that is the only motive for conversion. But let us also remember the Qur'ānic statement *ini-l-hukmu illa li-llāh* (Q. 12 : 40) — "Judgement is only God's"; do we then have the right to judge people? Man is a complex animal and all sorts of motives are involved in his actions. But we would hope that his motives for conversion would be pure, and we should try to examine them and be careful before admitting someone into our fold.

al-Faruqi: Formulating a code of missionary behaviour is not the first thing that we should be concerned with here. It is a second stage. The first stage must be the establishment of mutual trust. This requires the Christian missionaries who have been so far ahead of the Muslims in missionary work, and whose history of missionary activity over the last hundreds of years is full of incidents which create suspicion in the eyes of Muslims, to recognize that moral wrongs have been committed and to show their determination to take positive action to redress the situation. This must precede any attempt to sit down with Muslims to try to work out a mode of co-operation.

Ahmad: Dr al-Faruqi had made an important point: before we can proceed effectively in the matter of practical co-operation between Muslims and Christians, some sort of statement is needed from Christians repudiating past activities. I was much impressed by the statement produced by the Vatican in the recent dialogue with Muslims in Tripoli, Libya. It was a very clear, forthright statement. But I don't know of anything similar from the side of the Protestant churches, which have been in advance of the Catholic Church in missionary activity. All we have are the elusive references in the World Council of Churches' publications following earlier dialogues between Christians and Muslims.

Taylor: I think there are very explicit repudiations of proselytism, and very explicit statements on malpractice in mission in the WCC publications which are referred to. But the World Council of Churches cannot issue statements with the authority of the Vatican. Let me remind you all that the WCC is a consultative body, not a declaration-issuing body nor a legislative organization; but in its consultative nature, particularly through consultations such as this, we are able to stir up a lot of discussion.

Ahmad: I am sharing my feelings with you very frankly, but I feel bound to say that the Roman Catholic statement is frank, forthright and clear, while the references in the WCC documents seem to be couched in a language which has little relevance to past and present realities, and rather concentrates on hopes for the future. Furthermore, my worry is that the feedback from these documents to the Christian constituencies is very limited. The third thing that worries me is that the political dimensions of missionary involvement, of which we Muslims are very conscious — possibly over-conscious, I admit —, is not sufficiently clear in these statements.

Hajjar: We have been invited, first of all, to look back over history and to acknowledge that many mistakes have been made by Christians in the name of mission. As a Christian I don't deny that these mistakes have been made nor do I think that we should simply overlook them, because history is very much the mistress of our lives. We must take history very seriously if we are to look to the future. But it seems to me that in our present discussion we are erring by placing a unilateral blame upon the side of Christian mission. May I ask our Muslim brothers, particularly those of the Middle East, to recognize also how much wrong has been done to the Christians in the Middle East. I believe I am justified in asking this because, as a Christian in the Middle East, I have always upheld and defended the tradition of liberalism within Islam. If you want to ask for specific information I am ready to give it; but if you are ready to accept in principle that wrong has been inflicted upon the Middle Eastern Christians, then I am happy to proceed without specification. But if this principle is admitted, then it is necessary for acts of repentance to be reciprocal.

al-Faruqi: Unless there is real Christian repentance I don't think this conference will be of any avail. But apparently we are faced by forces that do not want to admit the moral wrongs and the mistakes.

Taylor: May I give a personal interpretation of what I understand to be implied in the term "reciprocal repentance". It does not mean that Christian repentance is conditional upon reciprocity. We are not making public our confessions to one another in order to make them conditional. Rather we are both conscious in a special way of being people who try to turn back to God in the sense of *tawbah* and *metanoia*. And it is because we are turning to God in this way that there could be a special quality in our relationship with each other. So we are sharing together a turning back to God, and this is the context of all our shared conversation about mission and *da'wah*.

Cragg: I find all this discussion, if I may say so, extremely desolating. I am not sure whether we realize the degree to which we are approaching this whole theme from within the vested interests of institutions, whether they be Muslim or Christian, the Mosque or the Church. Our whole thinking seems to be dominated by the priority of the institutional edifice, and our inter-relationship is seen rather in terms of a predatory exercise whereby one community is going to lose members to the other.

The real burden of mission is that truth should be known — truth as we hold it and live by it in our sincerity; we exist within a universal humanity to which we believe that truth relates. We are simply anxious that this truth should be accessible, not necessarily that it should be accepted.

All our discussion thus far is based on traditional institutional assumptions. But I think both sides are called to a sort of subjugation — we are not saying *Islāmu akbar* but *Allāhu akbar* (not "Islam is Greatest" but "God is Greatest"), just as within the Christian faith we are not saying "up with the Church", but that this is our report about the love of God in Christ, and this is what we want to share with others. Truth is there for recognition, and not for proselytism. I would have thought that the calling of this consultation itself is the recognition of the good faith which lies behind the World Council.

The complexes of history, and the institutional pride and bigotry, the complexities of human passion in institutionalized form which create the tragedies we all have in mind — these are all part of the evil tragedy in the human situation with which our various messages have to deal. It is the surmounting of this evil that we should be concerned with, in the context of a deep penitence, without creating a balance sheet of reciprocal wrongs. If I were to give details of the ways Christians have been wronged by Muslims, I feel that would be entirely counterproductive. It is our responsibility to transmute the tragic in history. The question before all of us is how do we build a world of peace? How does man break out of alienation into his true dignity? So many of the features in contemporary history seem to be leaving us behind — Muslims and Christians alike; the pressures of secularism, population, the earth's resources, the future of science — it is these areas of urgent challenge with which we should be dealing, rather than this bilateral concern which is based primarily on the desire for the survival of our respective institutions.

Ahmad: The institutional mentality which Bishop Cragg is criticizing comes up again and again, though I wanted to avoid it from the very beginning. I am afraid this institutional mentality is not the monopoly of any one group or community and it would be more profitable if everyone speaking in the name of religion does some honest heart-searching. Man has the capacity to rise above the level of vested interests and when we try to do that, to serve God, then alone real breakthrough becomes possible.

The idea of reciprocity in this context smacks of political bargaining and not of moral evaluation of a harrowing situation. If there is a single instance of Muslims' intolerance towards Christians, it puts me to shame — I would always be prepared to confess it and I am ready to do whatever I can to rectify that situation. But for God's sake don't compare such isolated incidents of human weakness with the enormous exploitation of the Muslims by the Christian world, through education, medicine, aid, etc. — all of which have been used as conscious and deliberate instruments of missionary policy. Please try to see into our hearts. We are trying to invoke the moral sense of our brothers so that we can make the world a better place to live in as human beings. In the deeper recesses of my heart I want every human being to be a Muslim. But I firmly believe that, if that is not possible, clearly this world would be a much better place to live in if Muslims become better Muslims, Christians become better Christians and Jews become better Jews — everyone going back to their religious traditions and meeting each other with greater reliance on their own spiritual sources.

🔲🔲🔲🔲🔲🔲🔲🔲🔲🔲🔲🔲🔲🔲🔲🔲🔲🔲🔲🔲🔲🔲🔲🔲🔲🔲🔲🔲🔲🔲🔲

STATEMENT OF THE CONFERENCE

The last day of the consultation was spent in the preparation of a final document for publication in the IRM along with the formal papers and excerpts of the discussions. In order to speed this undertaking two working papers were drafted, one by the Christians and the other by the Muslims, in which each group set out its consensus opinion. When the plenary session reconvened it was decided to adopt the more detailed Muslim paper as a basis for the combined document, and various revisions in the form of amendments, deletions and additions were then discussed and agreed. The participants requested the editors to undertake the technical editing of the final version which appears below.

The final document reflects some of the concerns and hopes felt by the participants. The participants were invited to Geneva in order to consult together as people experienced in Christian mission and Islamic da'wah, *and knowledgeable of each other's traditions, and it is in this spirit that the document seeks to draw together some of the main themes of the consultation, and to raise issues for the further consideration of interested parties.* (Editors)

Statement of the Conference on "Christian Mission and Islamic Da'wah" Chambésy, June 1976

1. In recognition that mission and *da'wah* are essential religious duties in both Christianity and Islam, a conference on Christian Mission and Islamic *Da'wah* was organized by the Commission on World Mission and Evangelism of the World Council of Churches, Geneva, in consultation with the Islamic Foundation, Leicester, and the Centre for the Study of Islam and Christian-Muslim Relations, Selly Oak Colleges, Birmingham, on 11 Jumada 28 - Rajab 4, 1396/June 26th - 30th, 1976. Beside examining the nature of mission and of *da'wah*, and the experience of each community of the missionary/*da'wah* activity of the other, the purpose of the conference was to promote reciprocal understanding between Muslims and Christians and to explore the means for a *modus vivendi* assuring the spiritual well-being of all.

2. The conference is in essential agreement that their respective communities, wherever they constitute a minority of the population, should enjoy a *de jure*

existence; that each religious community should be entitled to live its religious life in accordance with its religion in perfect freedom. The conference upholds the principle of religious freedom recognizing that the Muslims as well as the Christians must enjoy the full liberty to convince and be convinced, and to practise their faith and order their religious life in accordance with their own religious laws and principles; that the individual is perfectly entitled to maintain his/her religious integrity in obedience to his/her religious principles and in faithfulness to his/her religious identity.

3. The conference agrees that the family is a supremely precious and necessary institution. It expresses serious concern over the threats of disintegration and secularization facing the family institution, and it recommends that religious family law, whether Muslim or Christian, be not interfered with or changed in any way, directly or indirectly, by outsiders to their traditions. It also agrees that the family and community should have the right to ensure the religious education of their children by organizing their own schools, or by having teachers of their own denominations to teach religion to their children in the school, or by other suitable means. In any case they should be allowed to organize their cultural and spiritual life without outside interference, though with sensitivity to the situation in multi-religious societies.

4. The conference was grieved to hear that some Christians in some Muslim countries have felt themselves limited in the exercise of their religious freedom and have been denied their right to church buildings. The Muslim participants regard such violation as contrary to Islamic law as well as to the principle of religious freedom enunciated above.

5. The conference recognizes fully the right of Christians as well as of Muslims to other their corporate life in accordance with the injunctions of their own religious principles and laws, and to have and maintain all requisite institutions in accordance with their religious principles and laws as equal citizens.

6. The Christian participants extend to their Muslim brethren their full sympathy for the moral wrongs which the Muslim world has suffered at the hands of colonialists, neo-colonialists and their accomplices. The conference is aware that Muslim-Christian relations have been affected by mistrust, suspicion and fear. Instead of co-operating for their common good, Muslims and Christians have been estranged and alienated from one another. After more than a century of colonialism during which many missionaries served the interests of the colonial powers, whether deliberately or unconsciously, the Muslims have felt reluctant to co-operate with the Christians whom they have fought as agents of their oppressors. Although the time has certainly come to turn a new page in this relationship, the Muslims are still reluctant to take the step because their suspicion of Christian intentions continues. The reason is the undeniable fact that many of the Christian missionary services today continue to be undertaken for ulterior motives. Taking advantage of Muslim ignorance, of Muslim need for educational, health, cultural and social services, of Muslim political stresses and crises, of their economic dependence, political

division and general weakness and vulnerability, these missionary services have served purposes other than holy — proselytism, that is, adding members to the Christian community for reasons other than spiritual. Recently revealed linkages of some of these services with the intelligence offices of some big powers confirm and intensify an already aggravated situation. The conference strongly condemns all such abuse of *diakonia* (service). Its Christian members dissociate themselves in the name of Christianity from any service which has degraded itself by having any purpose whatever beside *agapé* (love for God and neighbour). They declare that any *diakonia* undertaken for any ulterior motive is a propaganda instrument and not an expression of *agapé*. They agree to exercise their full power and use whatever means at their disposal to bring Christian churches and religious organizations to a proper awareness of this situation.

7. The conference, being painfully aware that Muslim attitudes to Christian mission have been so adversely affected by the abuse of *diakonia*, strongly urges Christian churches and religious organizations to suspend their misused *diakonia* activities in the world of Islam. Such a radical measure is necessary to cleanse the atmosphere of Muslim-Christian relations and orientate them towards mutual recognition and co-operation worthy of the two great religions. The conference urges strongly that all material assistance donated by outside churches and religious organizations henceforth be distributed wherever possible through or in co-operation with the governments and local communities of people for whom they are intended, respecting the dignity and integrity of the people concerned.

8. The conference urges that soon after the measures mentioned in the two preceding paragraphs begin to be implemented, Muslims and Christians should be invited to an assembly representative of the two faiths to consider the methods of mission and *da'wah*, and the rules pertinent to each religion, and to seek modalities for enabling each religion to exercise its missionary call/*da'wah* in accordance with its own faith. The conference recognizes that mission and *da'wah* are essential religious duties of both Christianity and Islam, and that the suspension of misused *diakonia* services is to the end of re-establishing mission in the future on a religiously sound basis acceptable to both. Such an assembly may also establish permanent organs with Christian and Muslim participation for the purpose of preventing or dealing with aberrations or violations of Muslim/Christian understanding by either party.

9. The conference is aware that good neighbourly and co-operative relations between Christians and Muslims cannot exist or endure unless there is a deep-anchored reciprocal understanding of theologies, histories, moral and legal doctrines, social and political theories and problems of acculturation and modernization faced by the two faiths. To this end the conference urges that the World Council of Churches, the Vatican and the international Islamic organizations sponsor conferences at which these themes will be examined and discussed at regular intervals.

10. The conference, and especially the Muslim participants, express their deep and heartfelt appreciation to the WCC and the editors of the IRM for calling and sponsoring this conference. All participants express their joy that God has granted them the grace to bear in patience and empathize with one another. They are thankful to God that this conference may have made some contribution toward purifying the atmosphere of Muslim-Christian relations, and they pray that relations between their people may soon blossom into spiritual fellowship, to the glory of God alone.

GLOSSARY OF ARABIC TERMS

These terms either are not defined in the texts in which they appear, or recur at some distance from their first appearance and definition, without adequate context for reminding readers of their meaning. Editors

al-Haqq	the Truth
Rabb al-'Ālamīn	Lord of the Worlds
jannah	paradise
subhānahu wa ta'ālā	May He be praised and exalted
jahannam	hell
dā'iyah	missionary
īmān	faith
dīn al-fitrah	natural religion
fitrah	natural disposition
tarbiyah	education and training
tazkiyah	purification
Rahmān, Rahīm, Wadūd	The Merciful, the Mercy Giving, the Loving
jāhiliyyah	the ignoring of God
Allāhu akbar	God is greatest
jihād	spiritual and/or physical struggle to promote the cause of God
tajdīd	renewal and re-establishment
muftī	a recognized exponent of the Law
Ramadān	the month of fasting
shahādah	witness
salāt	the prescribed prayer
dār al-Islām	household of Islam
ahmadiyyah	19th/20th century movement founded in India by Ghulam Ahmad and now expanded across the world, but regarded by Muslims as outside Islam
nafs al-ammārah	the rebellious spirit (of man)
ummah	community
tawbah	repentance